# The Music Business

## (Explained In Plain English)

WHAT EVERY ARTIST & SONGWRITER
SHOULD KNOW TO AVOID GETTING
RIPPED OFF!

FIRST EDITION

**David Naggar, Esq.**
**Jeffrey D. Brandstetter, Esq.**

ISBN 0-9648709-0-8

Library of Congress Catalog Number: 96-96315

Cover and book design by Gary Hustwit.
Cover photo by Ted Drake.

Published by DaJé Publishing, 1824 Beach Street, San Francisco, CA 94123.


Printed in the USA.

# TABLE OF CONTENTS

# ACKNOWLEDGMENTS

No book is written in a vacuum. We have learned a great deal from all of the materials mentioned in this book. Additionally, we would like to acknowledge the assistance we've received from people throughout the industry, including Tom Chauncey of the Rosebud Agency, Kevin Coloff of Paramount Pictures, Erick Feitshans of Cinergi Pictures, Herbie Herbert of Herbie Herbert Management, Jim Kennedy of Windham Hill Records, George Scarlett of Tower Records, Howard Schomer of Winterland Productions and Ron Sobel of ASCAP.

# INTRODUCTION

## 1. THE BOTTOM LINE

Music is art. This book is *not* about art!

There is a harsh reality about the music business that you probably already know: **People (not counting loved ones) will help you if they think your art will make them money. They will not help you if they do not think your art will make them money.**

Like other businesses, the multi-billion dollar music industry is driven by money. If you are new to the music business, or have been involved for years but never really had the "big picture" explained to you in plain English, this book is for you.

We have written it to help artists and songwriters understand the basics of this industry beyond the club scene. You don't need to know everything, but if you don't understand the basics, you are setting yourself up to be ripped off.

We've used a lot of footnotes because we are lawyers and lawyers do that sort of thing. The information contained in the footnotes is important to clarify nuances, but is less important than the main text for an understanding of the "big picture." Also, we have tried to be specific about real numbers that are used in the industry, such as the royalty percentages earned by artists on record contracts and the royalty payment rate earned by songwriters for songs that appear on those records. Although we know these numbers are important to you, keep in mind that the numbers can change very quickly and many times over the course of your career. The concepts, however, remain the same and are the heart of the "big picture."

Let's get started...

# 2. SOURCES OF MUSIC INDUSTRY PROFITS

There are many different sources of profit for the musician and everyone else in the music business. Money is made from record sales, getting songs played on the radio, on television and in films, from concerts, merchandising, etc.

Today, for almost all performing artists, the real money flows first from making a record deal. In terms of money, successful record sales lead to everything else. The Recording Industry Association of America reported that in 1996, record sales were $12 billion dollars. Of course, the "catch" to participating in this bonanza is getting a good record deal in the first place.

If, as an artist, you haven't created a "buzz" in the industry, it is extremely unlikely that you'll get a good record deal. No one will think that they can make money from your art, and no one will spend the resources on you to see to it that you have a money-making record.

If you are a songwriter, your real money flows mostly from getting your songs on records. If the artist (or artist's representative) doesn't think that putting your song on their record will ultimately make them more money than not having your song on their record, then it won't be on their record. Don't count on <u>any</u> exceptions to this.

**Even though you may be both an artist and a songwriter, to follow the money flow, never confuse the terms "artist" and "songwriter."**

When we use the term "artist," we are talking about the person who performs the song, whether live or on a record, regardless of whether or not they wrote the song. When we use the term "songwriter," we are talking about the person who wrote the song, whether or not they perform it. Phil Collins as an <u>artist</u> and Phil Collins as a <u>songwriter</u> makes money in different ways for the performance of his songs (as an artist) and the writing of those same songs (as a songwriter).

Remembering this distinction is the most important key to understanding how you will make a living in the music business.

# BASICS FOR THE ARTIST

## 3. THE ARTIST'S BUSINESS ADVISORS

If you are an artist, there are three important advisors who will help you make key music business and career decisions: your personal manager, your attorney and your agent. There are good personal managers, attorneys and agents out there, but there seem to be many that are not. If you do not instinctively trust the person, do not deal with them.

The more high-powered, respected advisors you have on board, the more likely you are to get a record deal from a reputable record company.

### SPECIFICS ABOUT YOUR PERSONAL MANAGER

The personal manager is the most important member of the three because if you get a good one, a record company is going to feel comfortable that there is someone keeping an eye on your music business life for you. The record company is then more likely to think that you will generate income — i.e., record sales — for them.

A good personal manager will advise you regarding all aspects of your career. They are responsible for promoting you, advising you about what songs to record, who to hire as your producer, who to sign a recording contract with, and when and where to tour. They also coordinate publicity campaigns and insulate you from time demands such as interview requests. However, the personal involvement each personal manager actually provides varies greatly.

The vast majority of personal managers receive between 10% and 20% of the artist's gross earnings as compensation. The percentage is negotiable, and depends not only on the extent of service that will be provided, but on the experience of the manager as well. In our view, it is worth hiring the best personal manager available, without regard to the exact percentage being paid. We believe it is a better career move to part with 20% of gross earnings to hire a talented personal manager (one who can actively promote you and knows lots of people in the industry), rather than insisting on paying only 10% for someone who cannot further your career. When you become highly successful and the total dollars you earn grow wildly, you can then negotiate to lower the percentage a personal manager receives.

The term of a personal manager's contract is typically three to five years. Make sure your contract with a personal manager states that he or she will be the person primarily representing you, not someone to whom the manager delegates responsibilities. Your contract should also include a provision allowing you to cancel the contract if you are not earning a certain amount by a given date. Otherwise, you may be stuck for a long time with a personal manager who is taking you nowhere.

You should also be certain that the contract clearly states the amount of money your personal manager is to receive from earnings on deals you made during the term of the contract, but occurring after the expiration of the term. As an example, if you sign a deal to record ten albums with EMI, and soon thereafter have a falling out with your manager, should the manager receive 20% of all future profits? Clearly, that would not be fair. Limit the percentage amount and length of time after the termination of the contract that the manager is to receive payment.

Surprisingly, many of the industry's top managers do not have written contracts with their artists — just a handshake — and the only discussion point is the manager's percentage. All is left to good faith! While this may be a reality, it is <u>not</u> a good practice. As long as the relationship is going well, a handshake may be fine. But the moment things turn sour, you and your manager are likely to have very different ideas of what "the deal" was.

## SPECIFICS ABOUT YOUR ATTORNEY

Attorneys specialize in different fields of the practice of law. A great corporate attorney may know absolutely nothing about the music business. It is important to hire an attorney who is knowledgeable specifically about the music business because attorneys in the music business are heavily involved in negotiating and structuring the deals artists make. There are so many hidden pitfalls buried in the contracts used in this industry that hiring an attorney who understands the interplay between language and numbers is critical. One artist's 12% royalty on record sales may make the artist rich, while another artist's 12% royalty may pay that artist nothing.

As an artist, you must make sure you understand <u>in advance</u> how your attorney is going to charge you. Often, music attorneys use a retainer as a minimum payment against which they charge a flat hourly rate or "value" billing amount.[1] Expect to pay $200 an hour and up for a good music attorney in Los Angeles and New York, and a little less in Nashville, San Francisco and other major markets. Some music attorneys, if they believe in the artist or the artist is already established, will forego a set fee in exchange for a percentage of the artist's earnings that flow from agreements negotiated on the artist's behalf by the attorney (typically 5% to 10%). This latter option is worth considering if offered, but you have to weigh the option of not parting with a fixed amount of money now, against the option of parting with what could wind up being a lot of money down the road if you are very successful.

## SPECIFICS ABOUT YOUR AGENT

Music agents book concerts and other personal appearances. Music agents are not as powerful as their counterparts in the film and television business. We suggest that you allow your personal manager to help guide you in your decision when picking an agent, because it is your personal manager who will be dealing with the agent most of the time.

Just so you know, agents are regulated by unions: [2]

AFM (American Federation of Musicians) for instrumentalists.
AFTRA (American Federation of Television and Radio
        Artists) for vocalists and television actors/actresses.

---

[1] With "value" billing, an attorney charges you based on their estimation of the value of the services rendered to you. If they did good work for you, they assign a value to it. This is not a great system for you, but it is what it is.

[2] Other entertainment unions are EQUITY for stage performers and SAG (Screen Actors Guild) for film actors.

These unions each have their own printed form contracts that agents and agencies use.[3] With few exceptions, these unions allow agents to charge only 10% of an artist's gross earnings in the areas in which the agent renders services. Therefore, agents do not get a portion of the artist's income from records sales, songwriting or publishing. (AFM and AFTRA's printed forms actually do have a place for the artist to initial that give agents earnings from records; never agree to this.) Today, most music agents are anxious for business and discount the percentage of the artist's gross income they receive to well below 10% — between 5% and 7-1/2% is typical. If an artist is generating major income from concerts, the fee may be as little as 2-1/2% (or even less if the agent really wants a big name act on their roster).

Generally, agents will want you to sign a contract that lasts for three to five years. As an artist, try to limit the term of the contract to one year if you have the negotiating strength. This will allow you to move on if your agent is not performing well. It will also allow you to renegotiate a lower fee if you are generating major dollars.

There are many important terms to negotiate before selecting an agent. Your attorney and personal manager can help you with these. For instance, the scope of the agency must be understood. Is your agent in charge of lining up all concerts and personal appearances, or something less? Also, the geographic territory in which the agent represents you, and the specific duties of the agent in obtaining and negotiating the terms of your engagements, must be agreed upon. Even more esoteric items such as which union form governs when union forms overlap or

---

[3] If you sign with a major agency, they will have you sign agreements from all of the unions.

contradict each other must be negotiated. Make sure your attorney reviews the terms of your agency agreement. Otherwise, it could cost you a lot of money!

# 4. SENDING OUT YOUR MATERIAL

Many artists make the mistake of sending their tapes to everyone they know <u>before</u> creating any local interest in their music and <u>before</u> having any of their business advisors in place. This is not an effective way of getting "discovered." At a cost of $1+ per cassette, plus an additional $1+ to send it, you would be better off playing the lottery.

Until your music business advisors are in place, your demo tape cannot be shopped to the powers at a major record company in earnest. First, create a "buzz" about your music; <u>then</u> have a business advisor shop your tape.

As an artist, material you send directly to an established record company will generally not be listened to no matter how good it is. In part, this is because record companies fear potential liability in accepting material they have not asked for (what the industry calls "unsolicited" material). They do not want to be the target of a lawsuit by someone who later claims that their song was stolen and used by the record company.

Additionally, you should know that record companies receive more tapes and CDs than can properly be listened to. Therefore, the ones that actually do receive fair consideration are almost always professionally packaged, of high quality (sonic quality, not necessarily good music), and received from professional managers or music attorneys who are known to the key people at the record company.

Despite what we've said above, if you should choose to ignore our advice and send out your own material directly to record companies, then at the very least make sure that the material is "solicited,"[4] and send it to a particular <u>named</u> person in the Artists & Repertoire department of a record company (not "Attention: A & R director — Sony"). Also, include the following in every package: (1)a cassette tape with no more than three songs on it; (2)lyric sheets for all the songs; (3)a one-page "promo piece" including an introduction to the songs, a biography, press clippings and hype (only a little bit); and (4)a glossy photograph of you or the band. The more professional you and your materials look, the better. Today, image is as important in generating record sales as talent.

The only time that you, as an artist, will send your material to a publishing company is if you are also a songwriter. Publishing companies make money from owning rights to songs, not from signing artists. A major publishing company will not offer you (the songwriter) a publishing deal unless they are fairly certain that they can get you (the artist) a record deal, or unless they love your songs and you agree to have others record your songs. Once you've read this book, you will understand the economics of why that is. So, for an artist who is also a songwriter, the publishing deal often comes after the record deal is made.

If you want to be an artist, we recommend not signing a publishing deal until you are signed to a record deal or until you are convinced that you will not be signed to a record deal without a publisher's help (i.e., if you have been rejected by the record

---

[4] It is better to telephone in advance even those people who will accept "unsolicited" material to ask if you can send them your music. Making it "solicited" gives your material a greater chance of being heard in the best light possible. Call to confirm that your demo tape has arrived, and follow up with a call a couple of weeks later to confirm that it has been listened to. Remember though, if you do send out your own material, it is extremely unlikely to get serious consideration.

companies you want to deal with or can't even get your foot in the door).

A list of names, addresses and key people in the A & R Departments of most every established record company can be found in the *Recording Industry Sourcebook*, which is available in bookstores.[5]

---

[5] The *Recording Industry Sourcebook* is published every year. You can reach the folks who publish it at: 6400 Hollis St., Suite 12, Emeryville, CA 94608, tel. (510) 653-3307. (Cost: $75 per copy.)

# 5. RECORD COMPANIES AND DISTRIBUTION

The record business is cyclical. It does well in good economic times, and poorly in bad times. In good economic times, record companies fight over artists and make deals that are better for the artists.

First, a couple of definitions: A "record" is defined in the industry as <u>any</u> device that can transmit sound, including CDs, tapes and videos. An "album" is usually defined as 8-12 selections (songs), with approximately 35 minutes of playing time.

## RECORD COMPANIES

If an artist signs a recording contract with a record company, the artist will go into a studio and record songs for the record company. The record company then makes copies of the master recording and ships these records to a <u>distributor</u>. The distributor is the wholesaler who sells the records to the retail stores (like Tower Records, Sam Goody or The Wherehouse). The record company then gears up its advertising, promotions, sales, etc., and *voila*, everyone is working together toward the artist's stardom.

We tend to categorize record companies into four groups: major label record companies (with and without their own distribution capabilities), major label affiliate labels, independent labels (whose records are distributed through a major label) and true independent labels.

## MAJOR LABEL RECORD COMPANIES

The biggest record companies are called "major label" record companies. Many of these companies, such as Capitol, Columbia, Epic, Motown and MCA, are identified in the pages that follow. Take a look at your collection of cassettes and CDs. The better known artists are usually represented by major labels, and the major label's name will appear prominently on the cassette or CD.

Many divisions of a major label record company are important to an artist's success. Although your record deal will be negotiated with the Business Affairs Department (home of the lawyers), the most important departments for your success are the A & R Department, the Marketing/Sales Department(s) and the Promotions Department.[6] **If you and your personal manager are friends with the key people in these departments, you are much more likely to be successful. As Joni Mitchell says, it's "stoking the star-maker machinery behind the popular song":**

### 1) The A & R Department

People in the A & R ("Artists & Repertoire") Department act as the "ears" of the record company. They are the ones charged with finding new artists and working creatively with them. However, just because an A & R person loves your music and helps you sign a deal with the record company does not

---

[6] Not every major label record company has the same identical departments; nor do they identify their departments that serve particular functions by same name as other major label record companies.

mean that you are destined for stardom. Your record still has to be released, and it still has to sell. The path to glory is littered with artists who were already preparing themselves for stardom to strike after recording an album, only to discover that the record company decided not to release their album!

Understand that most of the people in the A & R Department of a major record company are not as important, in terms of deciding which artists get signed, as some would have you believe. Most of these people are under the age of 30 and are hired because they have convinced someone higher up in the company that they can spot and deliver talented artists to the record company.

The reality is that the dollar commitment a major label makes when they sign a new artist can be several hundred thousand dollars in recording costs, pressing and distribution, promotions, marketing, etc. Someone like David Geffen may hire someone to screen talented artists from the non-talented ones, but he and a few key advisors will be making most of the final decisions.

## 2) The Marketing and Sales Department(s)

These people are in charge of getting retail stores excited about carrying your record. They oversee album-cover artwork, promotional merchandise, advertising for your album, in-store displays and publicity.

## 3) The Promotions Department

The people in the Promotions Department are in charge of getting artists' records played on the radio. They do a lot of traveling and schmooze key radio station personnel to make sure your record gets played. If it doesn't get played, how is anyone going to know to buy it? The not-so-funny joke going around the industry nowadays is, "How can you tell if a record is going to be a hit? Look at the promo budget."

Some major labels have the ability to distribute their own records to stores. Some do not. (Distribution is discussed in the next subsection.) The major labels that do not distribute their own records generally distribute their records by using another major label's distribution arm. Majors without distribution capabilities use their brethren's distribution arms not only to keep their own overhead down, but also because these distributors have more power over record stores than independently owned distributors.

## MAJOR LABEL AFFILIATE LABELS

Major labels often have special relationships with smaller labels whereby the major label may fund the smaller label's recording and operating costs in exchange for part of the smaller label's profits. The line between a major label affiliate label and an independent label whose records are not funded by a major label but are distributed through them is often blurred.

## INDEPENDENT LABELS
### (Whose Records Are Distributed Through A Major Label)

These record companies have few, if any, full-time employees. An independent label signs artists and sees to it that the records are recorded. Often, it contracts with a major label to perform the promotion, marketing and many other paper-intensive functions of a record company. Many major label distributed independents earn their keep simply by finding talented artists and making sure that the major label record company actively markets and promotes those artists.

## TRUE INDEPENDENT LABELS

A true independent label has no association with a major label. True independents distribute their records through <u>independent distributors</u> not associated with the majors.

Which record company you choose to sign with is critical to your career. Do not go with the biggest just because it is the biggest. Your art may not get the full attention it needs to help you succeed. If the Marketing Department is busy pushing Michael Jackson, they may not have time for you. Meet with key members of the record company personnel who will be in charge of marketing and promoting your record before signing a deal. With an independent label, this may only be one person. Ask how they usually go about marketing and promoting an album. How committed are the key people to your album? Do they like your music? Will they push it even if it isn't initially successful? How much time and money are going to be spent marketing and promoting your album?

**Remember, you will not be signed unless the people at the record company believe your art will make them money. It does help if they like your music because if the people you are working with at the record company think you will make them money but do not really like your music, they will drop you**

**rather quickly from their roster if you do not make them money right away.**

Keep in mind that each record company is unique, and each has its own strengths in different styles of music. Since the "score-card" of who's who changes rapidly, the best way to know what services are offered by a particular record company is to ask (e.g., how they handle distribution, what resources are available to market and promote records, what success they've had getting radio airplay for their artists in the past).

## THE DISTRIBUTION SYSTEM

Major retailers, such as Tower Records, will no longer carry an artist's record in their stores unless the record has a distributor. In any event, a strong distribution system is critical to ensuring that enough of your records are going to be found in enough places to sell enough copies to make money for everyone involved in the process of making and selling a record. A fairly large retail record store can physically carry only 60,000 to 70,000 total CDs, but there are many more CD titles than this in print. Even if the store carried only one copy of every CD title, not every CD could be in every store. In reality, there will be many copies of a popular CD at every retailer, which means that there is even less physical space for even a single copy of many CDs.

This fact leads to one of the biggest advantages of signing with a fully-staffed major label, if you can. Major labels' records are distributed by large distributors, and large distributors are better able to get record stores to take their records. If a record store wants huge quantities of the latest Madonna record because it will sell and make money for the store, the distributor of Madonna's record has power over the store and can, shall we say, "strongly suggest" that the store might like to carry your record as well.7

After years of consolidation, only six "major" national wholesale distributors are left in the U.S., and all of them are owned by conglomerates that own the major label record companies:

**BMG**  (distributes Arista, BMG and RCA)8
**CEMA**  (distributes Capitol, EMI and Virgin)
**PolyGram**  (distributes A&M, Mercury and PolyGram)
**Sony Music** (distributes Columbia, Epic and Sony)
**UNI** (distributes Geffen, GRP and MCA)
**WEA** (distributes Atlantic, Elektra and Warner Bros.)

There are also a variety of smaller national and regional independent distributors. Because contracts between distributors and retailers generally allow retailers to return copies of records that do not sell, a distributor's cash flow can be erratic. All of the records a distributor thought they had sold to The Wherehouse or Sam Goody might come back to them a few months later. This is why some distributors are constantly on the brink of financial failure. Others are not particularly reputable. For example, five years ago, Tower had a vendor list of about 250 independent distributors. Today, only about 100 of

---

7 Large distributors require large distribution networks. They actually have more people working for them than a record company! As an example, Capitol Records has a little over 200 employees, but CEMA, its distribution arm, has over 600 employees.

8 Each of these "major" distributors distribute records for many other record companies as well. The Recording Industry Sourcebook contains a current list of the distributed labels of each "major" distributor.

these distributors are still in business. While some of the distributors merged operations, the vast majority simply went out of business. And of the 100 that are still in business, 40 owe money to Tower.

**If you are considering selling your own CD or tape through an independent distributor, make sure the distributor is in sound financial condition.** Here's an oversimplified example of what might be specified in the contracts between (1)you and the distributor, and (2)the distributor and the retailer, that explains why you need to be concerned: Suppose you "sell" your records to the distributor on January 15. Your contract with the distributor is likely to state that the distributor must pay you sometime in April. In the meantime, the distributor "sells" your records to Tower Records, for example. The distributor's contract with Tower will state that Tower must pay for your records sometime before the end of March (i.e., before the April date the distributor agreed to pay you). So far, so good.

But remember that in the music industry most contracts between a retailer and a distributor allow the retailer the right to return to the distributor any record that the distributor previously "sold" to the retailer that the public didn't buy.[9] If Tower decided in March to return to your distributor two thousand records of other artists which it could not sell to the public but for which it already paid the distributor in December of last year, then the distributor owes a refund to Tower on those two thousand records. Even if Tower actually sold all one thousand of your records to the public, since two thousand is more than one thousand, your distributor actually owes Tower money, not the

[9] A new record from a major label may stay in the store for 90-150 days before it will be returned to the distributor as unsold.

other way around. By April, the distributor will also owe you money for your one thousand records that were sold. You have been out of pocket the cost of making the CDs and tapes since January 15, but by the end of April, you may find that the distributor has paid for its own salaries and overhead but has no money left over to pay you. The moral is: check the distributor's financial statement before signing a contract with them!

Although it is usually better to have a major distributor distributing your records, depending on the style of your music or where you expect it to sell, this may not always be the case (if the independent is financially sound).

Independent distributors have less power over record stores, but may be better at specialized niche markets that majors can't be bothered with. For example, independent distributors are significant players in distributing rap music. Also, they can get product into their system and solicit orders within a few weeks. A major label record/distribution company can take up to 10 weeks to do the same thing.

There are different types of distributors, and not all distributors fit neatly into any one category. A traditional distribution entity buys from manufacturers (i.e., record companies) and sells directly to retail stores. These distributors also sell records to sub-distributors such as "One Stops" and "Rack Jobbers" who have niche markets:

## ONE STOPS

One Stops carry records from many record companies; hence, "one stop" shopping for the retailers who wish to purchase these records. One Stops sell records used in jukeboxes, and also sell to "Mom and Pop" retailers in small quantities. The markup to "Mom and Pop" retailers is higher than it is to bigger stores such as Sam Goody or The Warehouse.

## RACK JOBBERS

Rack Jobbers buy records from traditional distributors, and then sell the records in leased floor space within major department stores such as Wal-Mart and Sears. When you buy a record at Wal-Mart, you aren't really buying it from Wal-Mart.

♪ ♪ ♪

Record companies also license others to sell the record company's records to consumers, thereby bypassing the traditional distributor. Examples of such licensees are: (1)record clubs (e.g., buy 1, get 8 free); and (2)television packagers (e.g., Perry Como's Christmas Album, K-TEL).

Now that you have an idea of the record companies you might sign with and how your record might get distributed, let's discuss how an artist makes money from records.

# 6. ARTIST ROYALTY RATES AND PAYMENT CALCULATIONS

The most important contract in the entire music industry is the record contract. For making a record, an artist gets paid a portion of the money the record company takes in from record sales. This amount, which is negotiated between the record company and the artist, is known as the artist's royalty.

Having a basic understanding of the way in which royalty payments are calculated is critical if you are to understand the amount of money an artist can make from a record. In negotiating a record deal, an attorney who is familiar with the nuances of the music business and has a good sense of numbers really helps because as we stated earlier, one artist's 12% royalty may make him or her rich, whereas another artist's 12% royalty may yield them nothing.

A record company typically sells a CD or cassette to a distributor for approximately 50% of the suggested retail list price of the record ("SRLP"). As an example, a record company may charge a distributor $4.99 for a cassette with an SRLP of $9.98. (A distributor will take its own mark-up of 50¢ to $1, and sell the cassette to the retailer.)

Even though the record company collects only $4.99 for the cassette priced at $9.98, most major record company contracts state the artist's royalty rate as a percentage of the SRLP (of $9.98), not as a percentage of the wholesale price to the distributor.

Here are some typical artist royalty rates. The actual royalty rate, of course, will depend on the artist's negotiating strength. These royalty rates are the "base rates," and in many record contracts the rates are lowered if certain criteria are not met:[10]

For a new artist who has never had a record deal or a signed artist who has never sold more than say 100,000 albums of any record, a typical royalty rate will be 10% to 12% of the SRLP if they are signed to a major label record company. The spread is a bit wider if signed to an independent label. The typical range for an independent label is 9% to 13% of SRLP.[11]

An established artist whose last album sold 200,000 to 500,000 copies is likely to be able to negotiate a royalty rate of 14% to 16% of the SRLP.

A major star whose last album sold 750,000 copies or more can expect to command a royalty rate of 16% to 18% of the SRLP.

Royalties for "singles" rarely exceed 12% to 14%, and new artists are not likely to get even 10% of the SRLP unless a bidding war for their services breaks out.

---

10 Generally, the major labels apply the base rate only to records sold: (1)at full price; (2)in the U.S.; (3)on their main label (the majors have lesser labels and this can affect royalty payments); (4)through retail record stores; and (5)through a record company's normal distribution channels. Royalty rates for the same record are different depending on the method of distribution! The various methods and types of distribution are discussed in Chapter 7, "Other Artist Royalty Rates."

11 A few record companies, mostly smaller ones, calculate royalties as a percentage of the wholesale price they receive from the distributor. If this is the case in your record deal, the stated royalty percentages should be roughly double the royalty rate of the standard SRLP royalty rate that is discussed above. This is because the actual dollar payment to the artist who has an SRLP royalty rate of 10% (of $9.98), is the same to the one who has a wholesale royalty rate of 20% (of $4.99).

As you can see, the more sales the record company expects to generate from an artist's record, the higher the percentage they will be willing to pay the artist. Also, an escalated percentage of the SRLP on each individual album can be negotiated. For instance, the artist may receive only 12% on the sale of the first 100,000 units, 14% on the sale of the next 200,000 units and 16% on sales of units in excess of 300,000.

Now that you know the general royalty rate percentages various artists receive, you must understand that an artist doesn't actually get paid on their full royalty rate. By way of example, an artist with a cassette royalty rate of say 15% of the SRLP will not actually get paid 15% of $9.98 ($1.50) for each cassette sold. An artist's royalties from a gold album (i.e., one selling 500,000 copies) will definitely not generate $750,000 ($500,000 x $1.50) in artist's royalties. Not even close.

There are many deductions from the $750,000 found in every record company contract. But the amount of deductions each record company has in its form contract are not the same, and the deductions must be reviewed carefully. Let's look at some of the typical deductions.

## A REAL WORLD EXAMPLE OF A ROYALTY PAYMENT CALCULATION

(This stuff is a little dense. Alright, maybe more than a little dense, but it's important that you have an understanding of how this works.)

To start with, the record company will deduct a "packaging charge" off the top of the SRLP, from which the artist gets no royalty. Typically, the deduction is as follows:

10% deduction on vinyl records (now pretty much irrelevant);
20% deduction for cassettes and CDs.

Here's the step-by-step math for calculating cassette royalties:

| | |
|---|---:|
| SRLP of the cassette | $9.98 |
| Less: Packaging (20% of $9.98) | − $2.00 |
| | $7.98 |

So, if for example, an artist's royalty "base rate" is 15% of the SRLP for cassette sales, the artist's royalty would be $1.20 per cassette sold (15% of $7.98; not 15% of $9.98).

Most often, the artist's royalty rates are called "all-in," which means that the artist is responsible for paying his or her record producer out of the artist's share of royalties. Typically, the producer receives a royalty of 3% to 4% of the SRLP. Therefore, if the artist has to pay the producer his or her share from the artist's share (e.g., artist's share of 15% less 3% to the producer), the artist's remaining share is only 12% of $7.98 (96¢).

Also, "sold" is defined in an unusual way in the record business. Often, it turns out to be only 85% of records actually sold, so the artist actually receives only 96¢ on 85 of every 100 cassettes sold.[12] The artist gets no money on 15 of every 100 cassettes sold!

---

[12] This is because historically most record companies used to give retailers "free goods."

Continuing with the math:

| | |
|---|---|
| Assume 200,000 cassettes are shipped to the stores: | 200,000 |
| Times: Royalty per cassette that goes to the artist | x    $ .96 |
| Times: Royalty-bearing percentage | x      85% |
| | |
| Gross Royalty to the artist | $163,200.00 |

*Many record companies insist on paying only 80% to 85% of the royalty rate on CDs that they pay on cassettes. Although there seems to be no economic justification for this, it means that an artist who negotiates an "all–in" royalty rate of 15% for cassettes can probably expect to negotiate a royalty rate of 12% to 12-3/4% of the SRLP for a CD. Rather than lowering the royalty rate on CDs, some record companies deduct a higher packaging charge for CDs (often 25%).[13] This too has no economic justification.*

When calculating the amount of royalties to actually pay the artist, the record company withholds a part of what it may owe the artist. (That's right, you don't get the $163,200 yet.) They do so because contracts between distributors and record stores generally allow records "sold" by the distributor to the store to be returned to the distributor if the public isn't buying the record. Distributors receive the same type of "return privilege" from record companies.

This is important to you as the artist because <u>all</u> of your records can be returned if the public isn't buying them! The record companies and distributors argue that they do not know which records will come back to them even though computer tracking makes this less true today than ever before.

The money the record company holds back and does not pay the artist because of this return privilege is called a "reserve." Reserves may be held for as long as two years before they are finally paid to the artist.

Typically, a record company withholds paying an artist 20% to 40% of the royalties that would otherwise be due to an artist if the record store's purchase of the artist's CD or tape from the record company was final. The exact percentage is negotiable and depends on the artist's previous record sales track record. For rock artists and newer artists, a reserve of 30% to 40% is more common because a seemingly hot rock star's album may go cold in a hurry, and the record sales that a new artist can generate are unknown.

Continuing with the example of royalty payments from the previous pages:

| | |
|---|---|
| Gross Royalty (from above) | $163,200.00 |
| Less: 30% reserve (typical of a moderately | |
| successful rock artist) | − $  48,960.00 |
| | $114,240.00 |

As an artist, you may never see any of the $163,200, let alone the $114,240, because of "advances" and "recoupment" of advances.

Here's how advances and recoupment work: A record company often pays out money to the artist, or on the artist's behalf,

---

13 Also, some companies are using what's called an "up-lift" (130% of the wholesale price), instead of the SRLP, as the retail price on which they base the artist's royalty rate. This is done to further reduce the royalty payment actually received by the artist!

before records are sold and royalties are earned. This is called an "advance." For instance, the cost of going into the studio and recording the record is treated by the record company as an advance payment of record royalties to you. An advance is not only monies paid directly to the artist; it is also monies paid on the artist's behalf to the studio where the record is made, the producer and studio musicians. In some record contracts, the items considered "advanced" are painstakingly listed and can be a page long.

Typical dollar amounts advanced by a record company are as follows:

New artist signed to an independent record company
— $0 to $100,000
New artist signed to major label record company
— $100,000 to $200,000
A moderately successful artist — $200,000 to $400,000
Major star — $500,000 or more[14]

When money is made from selling a record, the record company keeps all of the artist's royalties to pay itself back before the artist gets paid anything. This is called "recoupment." The record company is recouping what it advanced the artist, and this may mean that the artist never actually receives any royalties from the record company, unless the artist's record is very successful.

---

[14] Often, when the artist has signed a record contract to record multiple albums, the advance to the artist for making any album other than the first one is stated as a percentage of the royalties earned from the artist's previous album. However, there is usually a minimum and a maximum that the record company will be obligated to advance irrespective of the actual sales of the previous album. The minimum protects the artist from a small advance if the previous album was a bomb, and the maximum protects the record company from paying a huge advance if the artist's previous album sells millions and millions of copies.

In our example, if the record company advances $150,000 to cover the costs of recording, the artist owes the record company $35,760 ($150,000 less $114,240), assuming the 30% reserve of the records "sold" to the record stores go unsold to the public and are eventually returned to the record company.

Not everything the record company pays for, however, is an advance. If the artist has negotiated his or her contract well, the following are not typically charged to the artist's account as an advance by the record company: manufacturing and shipping costs of a record, Marketing/Sales Department(s) expenses and Promotions Department expenses.

In addition, there are a few other deductions from the amount actually paid to the artist. While all deductions should be reviewed with your attorney before you sign any contract with a record company, the biggest ones you should be aware of are that no royalty payments are made on either (1)real free goods, or (2)promotional copies of records.

Real free goods are records given away by a record company to retailers as an incentive to get them to carry more of a particular record the record company is trying to push.

Promotional copies are given free by the record companies to radio stations and others in the industry who help promote records. They are not supposed to be for sale, but unfortunately, promotional copies often end up being sold.

If the royalty earned by the artist doesn't cover the amount of the advance (this actually happens a lot), the artist is said to be "in the red" and has a deficit. This amount is typically carried over to the next record through cross-collateralization, which means that the artist won't see any of his or her royalties earned as an artist from the next record (even if it is a hit) until the deficit from the first record is paid back to the record company in full. If there isn't a second record, the record company generally swallows the loss and the artist is no longer responsible for it.

**If you are an artist _and_ a songwriter, never allow the royalty payments due you as an artist from your record deal to be cross-collateralized with royalty payments due you as a songwriter for having written the songs on the album.** (Royalties earned as a songwriter will be discussed in next part of this book, which is about songwriter basics.)

So how much of a royalty does an artist make on a gold album? (Remember, a gold album is one which sells 500,000 copies.):

| | | |
|---|---:|---:|
| Cassette (suggested retail price) | $ | 9.98 |
| Less: Packaging (20%) | − $ | 2.00 |
| | $ | 7.98 |
| Times: Net royalty rate to artist (15% "all-in" less 3% to producer) | x | 12% |
| Gross Royalty per cassette (12% of $7.98) | $ | .96 |
| Times: 500,000 albums | x | 500,000 |
| SUBTOTAL | | $480,000.00 |
| Times: Royalty-bearing percentage | x | 85% |
| Gross Royalty | | $408,000.00 |
| Less: Typical recording costs/advances (some paid to the artist)[15] | − | $250,000.00 |
| TOTAL ROYALTY TO THE ARTIST | | $158,000.00 |

Not as much as you thought, eh? Note that because reserves are typically 20% to 40%, the artist will get only a fraction of the

$158,000 until perhaps two years later. A high royalty rate may be something people like to brag about at cocktail parties, but stated royalty rates are only part of the equation and can be misleading. If you are reviewing proposals from several record companies, compare the bottom line dollars going into your pocket, not the royalty rate itself.[16]

One final important point about the money that the artist actually gets to keep: the record producer's royalties are calculated somewhat differently. Remember, the producer's royalties are paid out of the artist's share of royalties. Traditionally, producer contracts state that the producer is not entitled to payment of his or her share of the SRLP until the artist's recording costs have been recouped by the record company. However, once the artist's recording costs have been recouped, the producer's royalties are owed immediately and must be actually paid to the producer for every record then sold.

In other words, if a record company was fully recouped when the sales of an album reached 300,000, the artist would finally actually receive money (the artist's percentage of the SRLP) on the next album sold. But when that album is sold, the producer is entitled to receive his or her share of the SRLP on all 300,001 albums sold! Because of this anomaly, and because the artist may

---

[15] Recording funds advanced to an artist to cover recording costs which are not spent are kept by the artist. But don't count on any money being left over unless you are a major star with a major budget.

[16] Royalty rates are often structured in ways that are much more complicated than our example above, but the principles are the same. For instance, many royalty rates are based on the sales of the previous album or on the average sales of previous albums. Also, the stated royalty rate for any given album may increase when certain levels of sales are achieved. For instance, the royalty rate might be 10% of SRLP for the first 100,000 albums sold, 11% of SRLP for the next 100,000 albums sold, 13% of SRLP for the next 100,000 albums sold, and so on.

still be "in the red" from a previous record (due to cross-collateralization), the artist can be responsible for paying the producer a lot of money even though the record company doesn't owe the artist a penny. **It is, therefore, generally a good idea to insist that the record company be responsible for paying producer royalties in the event of a shortfall.**[17]

Just so you know, many record companies will dictate to a lesser established artist who his or her record producer will be. Often, a record company chooses a producer based on how much the producer's "name" will help with marketing.

Typical advances for producers are as follows: Those working on an album with a budget of $150,000 expect to receive advances of $3,000 per master for each cut on the album (e.g., $30,000 per album if there are 10 songs on the album). Sought-after producers working on an album with a larger budget expect a much larger advance, as much as $10,000 per master or more. In addition, sometimes a separate "mixing fee" of $3,000 per master must be paid to the person who performs the final mix-down, blending the many tracks of a recording project down to two-track stereo, regardless of whether they are also the producer.

Many major label record companies are now directly advancing to the producer a portion of the recording costs that used to be advanced to the artist. This is especially true if the pro-

---

[17] Of course, the record company will extract other concessions for agreeing to do this, and will add the money it pays the producer to the amount "advanced" to the artist. Other than as noted above and in this footnote, producer royalties are generally calculated in the same way as artist royalties. The exception to this is for home videos. In that instance, the producer gets half of the customary royalty (on the theory that the audio — as opposed to the video — portion of the master is only half of the product).

ducer has his or her own studio. Even in this scenario, the money advanced to the producer is still "recoupable" from the artist's royalties before the artist sees a penny from record sales.

As we mentioned earlier, an artist's royalty rate on the same record varies depending on methods of distribution and sale. A more thorough list of the various royalty rates an artist receives is included in the next section.

# 7. OTHER ARTIST ROYALTY RATES

Actual payment to the artist of the following royalties is subject to the same deductions discussed in the previous section.

## 1) MID-LINE RECORDS

After the record has had its initial run in the current release and is no longer being actively promoted by the record company, it becomes a <u>catalog item</u>. Catalog items are sold to retailers at a reduced SRLP (60% to 80% of top-line new release records). Therefore, a record that is now a catalog item carries a reduced royalty payment (typically 75% of the artist's base rate discussed in the previous section).

## 2) BUDGET RECORDS

These records are sold to retailers at an even more reduced SRLP. You see them at the store at less than 60% of the price of top-line new release records. The artist's royalty rate on budget records is typically 50% to 66-2/3% of the base rate.

## 3) CUTOUTS AND DELETES

Cutouts and deletes are records taken out of the record company catalog because the record is <u>really</u> dead. Artists get no royalties for these. They are being sold at a loss. These are the records in the junk bins of record stores that we've all thumbed through hoping to find a great buy.

## 4) RECORD CLUBS

A record company contract will state that the record company has the exclusive right to "license" the recordings an artist makes for them. This means that if anyone wishes to use the recording, they must pay the record company a fee for the privilege. Record clubs pay record companies such a fee. Typically, the royalty rate received by the artist for records sold by the record club is 50% of the artist's base rate, but there is usually a cap on the total royalty payment such that the record company never has to pay the artist more than 50% of the licensing fee the record company receives from the record club. There are also substantial reductions in royalty payments owed to the artist for any of his or her albums which are given free to the record club by the record company. Record company "freebies" can equal the total number of albums of all artists sold by the record company to the record club. This means that a particular artist can get burned if the record company designates all of his or her albums to be freebies.

## 5) COUPLING AND COMPILATIONS

Coupling occurs when two or more artists appear on the same album. When many artists appear on the same album, the album is sometimes called a compilation album. The total royalties generated by such albums are split among the artists.

## 6) SAMPLERS

Samplers are a form of coupling. Generally, they are low-priced albums in which a few new artists are featured. There is no royalty payment because these records are sold by record companies as promotions.

## 7) PREMIUMS

These are records sold in conjunction with other products, such as cereal. The royalty rate is typically 50% of the base rate, but the rate is not a percentage of the SRLP; rather, it is a percentage of the actual price at which the record is sold to the advertiser. The artist should try to limit this type of record sale from occurring without the artist's consent.

## 8) FILM SOUNDTRACK ALBUM

The artist's record company may grant a film company a license to use the record company's artist's performance of a song in the film company's soundtrack album. The artist's royalty rate is usually 50% of the record company's licensing fee.

## 9) HOME VIDEO SALES

Generally, the royalty rate is 10% of the wholesale price of the video.

## 10) GREATEST HITS ALBUM

An artist's royalties for a "Greatest Hits" album are based on a blended rate of the royalty rates the artist received from the albums on which each song first appeared.

## 11) FOREIGN ROYALTIES

These vary widely depending on the artist's recognition in a particular country. In Canada, the royalty rate is typically 85% of the base rate. In industrialized nations such as the United

Kingdom, France, Italy, Germany, Japan and Australia, the royalty rate is typically 60% to 75% of the base rate. In what is referred to in a typical record contract as "Rest of World," the royalty rate is typically 50% to 60% of the base rate.

## 12) PUBLIC PERFORMANCE OF MASTER

In many foreign countries, money is paid by radio stations to the record company for playing the record. Radio stations in the U.S. do not make such payments to the record company. U.S.-based record companies have typically refused to pay the artist any additional royalties for foreign performances, although with the growth of the international market, requiring payment for these performances is increasingly becoming worth fighting for.

# 8. KEY RECORD CONTRACT DEAL POINTS

Now that you have a sense of the royalty numbers, the key points of a record contract discussed below will make more sense to you. They all deal, to one extent or another, with whether money ends up in the artist's pocket or in the record company's pocket. To discuss each at length would make this book far too long and would probably bore you to death. Also, we have not discussed issues regarding your creative freedom and control. These you already know enough about to negotiate wisely.

Keep this list as a handy reference for when you are negotiating or renegotiating your record deal. Make sure you discuss each point with a good lawyer.

## 1) ROYALTY RATES AND CALCULATIONS

As we discussed previously, an artist makes money from the record company by receiving royalties from the record company. The more records you sell, the higher your royalty should be. Hopefully, we have given you a good understanding of how this works.

## 2) LENGTH OF CONTRACT/OPTIONS

Generally, major labels insist that a new artist sign a contract that lasts nine months after the artist has delivered one completed album. Major label record companies also insist on receiving anywhere from three to nine consecutive "options" to extend the term of the contract. As an artist, these options may require you to make many albums at a reduced royalty rate. In our opinion, every effort should be made to limit the number of options the record company has to extend the term of your contract to four or less. The original contract should contain a clause that states the royalty payments due for each album recorded under subsequent option periods. The artist's attorney should negotiate for higher royalty rates for each new album recorded.

## 3) RELEASE OF THE RECORD

Just because an artist signs a record deal and makes an album does not mean that the album will be released or distributed, unless the artist negotiates this into his or her contract with the record company. The release of the album should be guaranteed by the record company, or at the very least, the contract should allow the artist to go elsewhere if the album is not released. Also, in the case of a major label, the album should be released on the record company's main label, not some smaller label they just acquired or are starting.

## 4) PROMOTION & INITIAL RUN OF THE RECORD

It is critical that your record receives adequate promotion or it will die. You should attempt to get the record company to commit to a certain dollar amount that will be expended on the promotion of your records to radio stations. If they will not do so, you must question their commitment to you.

Additionally, if there is a bidding war for your services, you should attempt to get the record company to commit to hire "independent promotion" people on your behalf. These people are well-connected with radio station programmers, but are not part of the record company's Promotions Department. You also want to limit how much of what a record company pays to an independent promoter is recoupable by the record company.

The initial run of the record before it becomes a catalog item should be at least 12 to 18 months.

## 5) TOUR SUPPORT

Record companies want you to tour because doing so sells records. Many tours are actually money losers. We discuss this in greater detail in Chapter 19, "On Tour." If your tour is a money loser, generally 100% of the costs advanced by the record company for the tour are recoupable by the record company. Try to get the record company to guarantee tour support, at least for your first tour.

## 6) VIDEOS

Provisions in record contracts regarding music videos are growing in length as the importance of videos to music industry profits grows. Today, music videos themselves are money losers, but having a video is increasingly important to achieving high record sales. If you enter into a deal with a major label, it is imperative that the label provide the funds to make the video. Typically, a record company will agree to charge 50% of the cost of making a video as recoupable against the audio (i.e., the record) and 50% against the sale of videos.

# 7) LIMITATIONS ON COUPLING AND COMPILATIONS

Try to limit the record company's ability to force you to participate in these arrangements. They may be good for the record company in the short run and bad for your career in the long run. You should control your image, not the record company.

# 8) ALBUM COVER ARTWORK

Speaking of "image," who controls the album artwork is negotiable. This can be important not only for your image, but also in determining whether you or the record company profits from merchandising associated with the artwork.

# 9) TERRITORY

For less established artists, a record company's "territory" is usually defined as the entire "universe." This means that the record company can sell your records anywhere. You may wish to limit a record company's territory if they are unable to effectively market your album somewhere. For instance, if you expect your music to be especially popular in Japan, it is important that the record company which sells your music in Japan can do so effectively. As more and more records are sold outside of the U.S. and Canada, the extent of a record company's territory is apt to be negotiated more heavily in the future.

## 10) RESERVE LIMITATIONS

Try to negotiate the "reserve" percentage down as best you can. Also, try to limit the amount of time a record company can hold on to the reserve once it knows that your records were actually sold to the general public.

## 11) CONTROLLED COMPOSITION CLAUSE

In a typical record contract, the money you earn for writing songs that appear on a record is reduced if you are the artist on the record. This limitation is contained in the controlled composition clause of a record contract. You need to understand how songwriters get paid (covered in the next part of this book) in order to understand this clause. It is a critically important part of the artist's record deal.

## 12) ACCOUNTINGS AND AUDITING RIGHTS

Be sure that your contract requires periodic accountings from the record company that detail your record sales, expenses charged to your account, and royalty payments. Also, insist that the contract allow you to conduct a detailed audit of their numbers. The more rights you have, the better. This can help prevent the record company from becoming sloppy with your account.

# 9. INDEPENDENT LABEL DEALS WITH MAJOR LABELS

Throughout most of the 1980s, the major label record companies bought out most of the worthwhile smaller labels. As the cost of recording a viable record comes tumbling down, new independents are constantly cropping up. Many of them are nothing more than artists' own "vanity" labels, yet if there is the potential for successful national distribution, a distribution deal may be struck with a major record label.

While there are <u>many</u> different types of deals that are entered into between independent labels and major label record companies, they tend to fall into three categories:

## INDEPENDENT PRODUCTION AGREEMENTS

An Independent Production Agreement is the agreement an independent label signs with the major label record company to manufacture, distribute, market and promote the record of an artist already signed to the independent label.

The agreement calls for the major label record company to give the independent label a 1% to 5% higher royalty rate than it does on deals done directly with artists, but there is usually a cap on the total payment amount to the independent label. The more services the independent label provides by way of marketing and promoting its artist(s), the higher the royalty rate the independent can negotiate for itself. The independent retains responsibility to pay the artist(s) their royalties.

If the major label is enamored with the owner of an independent label (e.g., a powerful record producer), or several of the artists controlled by the independent label, an agreement covering all the artists of the independent label may be entered into.

## PROFIT SPLITTING

Sometimes, rather than entering into an independent production agreement, the independent and major label enter into an arrangement in which the workload and profits are split between them. Under one scenario, the major label may pay for manufacturing and arrange for distribution. It would then charge the independent for all of the costs and retain a percentage of the profit. If the record is ultimately only moderately successful, it is probably better for the independent label to have an independent production agreement. If, however, the album is highly successful, it is better for the independent to have a profit-splitting arrangement.

## STRAIGHT DISTRIBUTION DEALS

If an independent label wants to gamble, they may enter into a deal with a major label's distribution arm to distribute records for the independent label strictly as a wholesaler. This means that records are sold to the major distributor at a wholesale price, and the distributor marks up the wholesale price before selling it to the record store.

For example, from a wholesale price of $4.99 (for a cassette that retails for $9.98), the independent must pay all of the manufacturing costs, overhead, artist royalties, mechanical royalties to songwriters and publishers, promotion and marketing costs, and any other costs. Whatever is left over is the independent's profit.

# BASICS FOR THE SONGWRITER

## 10. COPYRIGHTS — PROTECTING YOUR SONGS

Remember, the _artist_ is paid a royalty from the record company for being the artist on their record. Most often, the artist's royalty rate is a percentage of the suggested retail list price of the record (less a whole bunch of deductions). The person who actually writes a song, whether or not they are an artist, makes money under different arrangements for having written the song.

To understand how money is earned by the songwriter, you must first know a little about copyrights.

### YOUR COPYRIGHT MONOPOLY

In the U.S., a copyright is a limited duration monopoly given by the government to the songwriter.[18] As the songwriter, you own a monopoly as it relates to your song. You are Mr. or Ms. "Big," and you call the shots.

---

[18] Technically, the "originator" of the song gets the copyright. The originator may not be the songwriter if the songwriter agreed to write the song as a "work for hire." See the section in this chapter entitled "Works Made For Hire." This comes up most often in connection with film scores and television background music. See Chapters 22 and 23.

To obtain this copyright monopoly, the song (the "work" as it is called by the Copyright Act) has to be "original" and "of sufficient materiality." There are no specific legal tests that define what is original or what is of sufficient materiality. If there is a legal fight about whether a song is "original," a judge or a jury will ultimately determine the issue based in part on their subjective views.

As soon as a "tangible" copy of your song is made, a copyright exists. A tangible copy of a song exists once you have created something you can touch, like a tape or a lead sheet.[19] Technically, you don't have to file anything with the government to obtain a copyright!

Once the copyright exists, the songwriter[20] by law is granted, among other rights, the exclusive rights to: (1)reproduce the work (e.g., record the song); (2)distribute copies of the work; and (3)perform the work publicly.[21] This means that no one can do any of the above without the songwriter's permission. By registering a copyrighted song with the U.S. Copyright Office in Washington, D.C., the songwriter[22] can collect compulsory license royalties (discussed in the next subsection), or sue for infringement and collect the fair market value of use and the infringer's profits.[23]

---

[19] A "lead sheet" is a sheet of paper that typically contains the melody, chords and lyrics of a song.

[20] See footnote 18.

[21] Further rights are listed in §106 of the Copyright Act of 1976.

[22] Your publisher may be the one registering the copyright with the Copyright Office if you have transferred copyright ownership to your publisher.

# Infringement

It is considered "infringement" for a songwriter to use a portion of someone else's copyrighted song in a new song without permission unless the new song is a "fair use" of the copyrighted song, such as often is the case with a parody. Whether a particular use of a portion of someone else's song constitutes "fair use" depends on a number of factors, including how much of the copyrighted song is used, in what context it is used, and whether the use of the copyrighted song will deprive the copyright owner of future profits.

Obviously, infringement of an existing song defeats copyright protection in the newer song. The legal test is simply whether the amount taken from the older copyrighted song (music or words) was "substantial." This loose standard is applied by the judge or jury when listening to the songs and comparing them.

# Joint Works

Joint works are those songs that are written by two or more people. If two or more songwriters intend to merge their individual contribution at the time of a song's creation, the writers have created a "joint-work." Each songwriter has the right to license the entire song, subject to paying the other songwriter(s)

---

23 Legal issues surrounding copyright infringement can be complex, with many such issues still being decided by the courts. "Sampling" (i.e., digitally recording a small portion of an existing song), for example, is currently determined by a fairly open-ended standard: if the sound sampled was so distinctive and unusual to be thought of by a judge or a jury as "original," anyone who samples the sound and uses the sample as part of a new song may be guilty of infringement.

their share of the royalties, because each owns an undivided interest in the copyright of the entire song.[24]

Even if the writers create separate parts, as when one writes the music and the other writes the lyrics, each is a co-owner of the indivisible whole of the joint work. If, for example, the original lyrics are later completely rejected and a new songwriter writes new lyrics, the original lyricist still owns a part of the new song! This new song is called a "derivative work."[25]

If you want to avoid having someone claim that their contribution to your song was intended to create a joint work, make it clear up front. You do not want any other person claiming an interest in your copyright. For instance, when you are making a demo tape with the help of a producer or arranger, always clarify that his or her services are being rendered as a producer or arranger, and not as a songwriter.

## Arrangements

Arrangements of songs rarely qualify for copyright protection. Under the Copyright Act, arrangements are copyrightable only if the arrangement was made by the copyright owner of the song or the copyright owner of the song consents to allowing the arrangement to be copyrighted. So, just because your song is recorded in someone else's studio and they help you produce

---

[24] This is discussed in §201(a) of the Copyright Act of 1976.

[25] Technically, a derivative work is a song (or other "work") which is created by the making of modifications or additions to a preexisting work. In the example above, the original lyrics and melody form the preexisting work, while the new songwriter's lyrics together with the original melody comprise the derivative work. If the original lyricist uses the original lyrics with a new melody, it too is a "derivative work."

or arrange your song by adding key instrumental tracks and helping you "phrase" the song just right, does not mean that they are entitled to a copyrightable interest in either your song or the arrangement of your song.

## Works Made For Hire

"Works made for hire," also known as "works for hire," refers to songs written by a songwriter either as an employee or as an independent contractor for someone else. The person or entity who does the hiring, not the actual songwriter, is the "originator" and "author" of the song, and therefore owns the copyright. The royalties generated by a song belong to them, not to the actual songwriter, unless the "work for hire" agreement specifically grants the songwriter an interest in royalty income.

## EXCEPTIONS TO YOUR COPYRIGHT MONOPOLY

There are several exceptions under the Copyright Act to a songwriter's "exclusive" monopoly rights. The most important one involves the use of a song on a record.

A license to use the song must be granted by the copyright owner if all of the following are true: (1)the song is a "nondramatic" musical composition;[26] (2)the song has been previously recorded and distributed publicly in phonorecords with the copy-

---

[26] The law does not give the words "dramatic musical composition" clear meaning. You can assume that your song is a "nondramatic musical composition," unless it is written specifically for a musical or an opera. However, even if your song is written for a musical or an opera, it might still be considered a "nondramatic musical composition" if it is later used in a nondramatic fashion (e.g., played on the radio).

right owner's permission;27 and (3)the requested license is for the use of your song in phonorecords only.

The license that must be granted if all of the above is true is referred to as a "compulsory mechanical license," and is the major basis upon which payment by record companies to songwriters and publishers is calculated. If a record company wants to take advantage of a compulsory mechanical license to use your song, it must pay you a royalty in exchange for it.

Note that there is <u>no</u> compulsory license for songs used in movies or home videos! If you do not want your song to be used in a movie, it can't be used.28 As such, you are free to charge the film company whatever you want (or whatever they are willing to pay).29

## THE COPYRIGHT NOTICE

Legally, you don't have to put any copyright notice on demo tapes since demos aren't "published," but we recommend that you do it anyway because it appears more professional. Here's how:

The symbol for a notice of copyright in a song is ©, and the symbol for a notice of copyright in a sound recording is ℗.

---

27 Pursuant to the Copyright Act, "phonorecord" means every form of recording (CDs, tapes, etc.) <u>except</u> recordings "accompanying a motion picture or other audiovisual work."

28 Other compulsory licenses involve cable television, public television (PBS) and jukeboxes.

29 This is pursuant to §115 of the Copyright Act of 1976.

If you are protecting anything that is "visibly perceptible" (i.e., you can see it), use the symbol ©. You should use this symbol on lead sheets, J-cards, sheet music, and albums (if lyrics are printed and to protect the "artwork"). For example, on our lead sheets, we would put:

© 1997 Jeffrey D. Brandstetter & David Naggar
All rights reserved.

If you are protecting the sound recording itself (which is not visibly perceptible), use the symbol ℗. Put this notice on the surface, label or container of the cassette or CD. If your cassette or CD has artwork that you wish to protect, add the symbol ©. On our cassette or CD, we would put:

© ℗ 1997 Jeffrey D. Brandstetter & David Naggar
All rights reserved.

For a copyright notice to be effective, you must include: (1)the letter C or P inside a circle; (2)the year of "publication" (publication generally occurs when the song is distributed to the public); and (3)the name(s) of the copyright owner(s). All three must be included. Because the words "All rights reserved" historically added protection in certain South American countries, they too should be added.

## COPYRIGHT REGISTRATION FORMS

Although material can be protected by simply using the © or ℗ symbols, in order to collect compulsory license royalties or sue for infringement, a copyright must also be registered with the Copyright Office. The fee is $20 per registration, but you can register a collection of your songs as one "work" and save a lot of money. To obtain the forms necessary to register a copyright, telephone the Copyright Office at (202) 707-3000, or write to: Information and Publication Section LM-455, Copyright Office, Library of Congress, Washington, D.C. 20559.

## THE DURATION OF A COPYRIGHT

A copyright for works created after January 1, 1978 is valid for the life of the last surviving author plus 50 years.

Copyright protection for works first published and registered with the Copyright Office between January 1, 1964 and December 31, 1977 is valid initially for 28 years. There is an automatic renewal of the copyright protection for an additional 47 years at the expiration of the 28 year period.[30] Thus, the total copyright protection is 75 years from the date of publication.

Copyright protection for all works published before January 1, 1964 has either expired (which means that the works are in the public domain and anyone can use them for free),[31] or has already been properly extended with the Copyright Office (which means that the copyright is valid for 75 years from the date of publication).[32] In other words, anyone can freely use any song written before 1922 (i.e., over 75 years before 1997), and any work written between 1922 and 1963 for which a proper

---

[30] Because of burden of proof issues that arise in a court of law if the validity of the copyright is ever challenged, it is better practice to actually file a renewal notice.

[31] Once a song is in the public domain, the copyright owner is no longer entitled to any royalty payment.

[32] The duration of a copyright on works for hire is the lesser of 75 years from publication or 100 years from creation.

application to extend copyright protection was not filed with the
Copyright Office.

Now that you know how to protect your songs, let's discuss
sending your out demo tapes.

# 11. SENDING OUT YOUR SONGS

As a songwriter, your goal is to get your songs on a record.

If you do not have an active publisher, material you send directly to anybody who can actually help you earn money from your song (including a publisher) will generally not be listened to no matter how good it is, unless it is first solicited. People in the business are afraid to be the target of a frivolous lawsuit by someone who later claims that their song was stolen.

Initially, it is best to have someone in the business end of the music industry, such as a music attorney, send out your material because it lends more credibility to your songs. A *great* song can, however, occasionally speak for itself, even if it does come directly from you.

**If you do send out your own tapes, you should try to send them to those who are as close to the decision-making source as possible!** If an artist is established, the artist, their personal manager, or the producer of the artist's last album, is <u>much</u> more likely than a publisher or an A & R representative to ultimately decide what goes on the artist's record.

If, on the other hand, an artist is unknown and newly signed, the record company is likely to dictate which songs ultimately appear on the artist's record. Remember though, if you haven't received permission to send your demo, it probably won't be listened to by anybody. Here are some of the better sources we've discovered to help a songwriter send a demo to the right place:

## *Pollstar*

POLLSTAR, 4697 W. Jacquelyn Ave., Fresno, CA 93722; tel. (800) 344-7383, in California (209) 271-7900. POLLSTAR concentrates on providing concert tour information, but subscribers also receive "Contact Directories," which include record company rosters, music radio directories and agency directories. The Contact Directory that we find most valuable is the one directory <u>not</u> included in the cost of the subscription. POLLSTAR calls it the "Confidential Artist Management Roster." The Roster gives current phone numbers, fax numbers and addresses of artists' managers. (Current cost: $97.50 for the Confidential Artist Management Roster if you are a subscriber and $140 if you are not; $295 for an annual subscription.)

## *Billboard International Talent And Touring Directory*

Billboard Directories, P.O. Box 2016, Lakewood, NJ 08701; tel. (800) 344-7119. This guide, published annually, lists hundreds of artists, together with booking agents, personal managers and record companies. There is also a section on where to contact the agents and managers. (Current cost: $99.)

## *Yellow Pages Of Rock*

Album Network, 120 N. Victory Blvd., Third Floor, Burbank, CA 91502; tel. (818) 955-4000. This publication lists the names, addresses and phone numbers of record companies, managers, agents, attorneys, publicists, retailers, publishers, record distributors, radio stations, etc. (Current cost: $131 in California.)

## *The Official Country Music Directory*

Entertainment Media Corp., P.O. Box 7000, Rancho Mirage, CA 92270; tel.(800)395-6736 or (619)773-0995.This directory, published annually, is devoted exclusively to <u>country</u> music. It lists the names, addresses and phone numbers of country artists, their personal managers, booking agencies, record companies, etc. (Current cost: $125.)

Also, important tidbits can often be found in the major industry trade magazine, *Billboard.* Other good sources of information are *Radio and Records, Cashbox* and *Hits Magazine.* (For example, every year, the August issue of *Hits Magazine* lists the phone numbers of many artists' managers with cross-references to the artists. It doesn't give addresses though.)

# 12. PRIMARY SOURCES OF INCOME

A *songwriter* makes money by selling, generally through his or her publisher, rights to use one or more of the songwriter's songs. In most circumstances, in order to get paid, a publishing entity which owns the legal copyright to the song must be specified. A songwriter may act as his or her own publisher. (See Chapter 16, "Creating Your Own Publishing Company.") Often, however, the songwriter can generate substantially more income from a song by associating with a major publishing company.

Profits generated from a song are split between the songwriter and the publisher (even if you act as your own publisher). Through quirks of history, the holder(s) of the publisher's share (regardless of who owns the "publishing" — i.e., the copyright rights) are generally said to receive 50% of the song's profits. The remaining 50% is said to be the writer's share. Notwithstanding the use of the terms publisher's share and writer's share, the actual profits split between a songwriter and a "real" publisher vary greatly depending on the arrangement between them. Very often, the songwriter receives a large portion of the publisher's share. Therefore, in this chapter we will discuss the total money generated by a song. We will discuss the role of publishers in more detail in Chapter 14.

The two primary sources of income for songs are: (1) "mechanical" royalties paid by the record company for using the songwriter's song on one of its records; and (2) "performing" royalties paid by television stations, radio stations, night clubs, restaurants, etc. for playing the songwriter's song publicly. Note that "performing" royalties are not paid by artists for performing a song.

# 1) MECHANICAL ROYALTIES

In exchange for mechanical rights (i.e., the rights to reproduce a song in records), record companies pay mechanical royalties to the copyright owner of a song. The copyright owner is the songwriter or any person or entity to whom the songwriter assigns the legal copyright ownership.

The amount of the payment is negotiated between the record company and the copyright owner. However, if the criteria discussed in the "Exceptions To Your Copyright Monopoly" section of Chapter 10 are met, a copyright owner must license his or her song to any record company that agrees to pay the compulsory mechanical license rate set by statute. Currently, the rate per song is the larger of (1)6.95¢, or (2)1.3¢ per minute of playing time (or fraction thereof) for each record sold.

For example, if your 3-minute song was licensed to a record company under the terms of a compulsory mechanical license for use on an album that sold 100,000 copies, a record company would be obligated to pay the copyright owner $6,950 (100,000 x 6.95¢) in mechanical royalties.

If your 6-1/2-minute song was licensed to a record company under the terms of a compulsory mechanical license for use on an album that sold 2,000,000 copies, a record company would be obligated to pay the copyright owner $182,000 (2,000,000 x 1.3¢ x 7) in mechanical royalties.

If you co-wrote four 3-minute songs with a friend, and each of the songs was licensed to a record company under the terms of a <u>compulsory</u> mechanical license for use on an album that sold 500,000 copies (a gold album), a record company would be obligated to pay the copyright owners $139,000 (500,000 x 4 songs x 6.95¢) in mechanical royalties. You and your publisher (the owners of an undivided 1/2 interest in the copyright) would receive $69,500 (half of the $139,000). Your friend (and his or her publisher) would receive the other half.[33]

Of course, record companies do not want to pay the full statutory amount, and so they attempt to negotiate agreements with copyright owners that call for payment of a reduced rate. If they do not agree to pay the full statutory amount, however, the copyright owner can refuse to allow the record company to use the song.

The predominant way in which a record company forces a reduction in the amount of mechanical royalties it has to pay a songwriter is contained in the <u>controlled composition clause</u> of a record contract between the artist and the record company.

A "controlled composition" is a song written, owned or controlled, in whole or in part, by the artist. Since, unlike <u>artist</u> royalties, the record company cannot "recoup" anything from a <u>songwriter's</u> mechanical royalties,[34] record companies typically

---

[33] Compulsory mechanical licenses are hardly ever used! It is easier for a copyright owner to monitor direct licenses. It is also easier for record companies to deal with direct licenses because the compulsory accounting rules are considered too time-consuming. The statutory compulsory mechanical license rate is important because it sets the standard for the mechanical rates that record companies actually do pay.

[34] Money isn't "advanced" by the record company to the songwriter in the same way it is advanced to the artist.

insist that the artist (with the exception of major stars) agree to license songs that are controlled by the artist for 75% of the minimum statutory rate. In other words, no matter how long the song is, the record company will pay only 5.21¢ (75% x 6.95¢). Often, they pay only 3.475¢ (50% x 6.95¢) for mid-line and budget records. Also, the controlled composition clause will limit the record company's total mechanical royalty payments on any album to either (1)the number of songs actually on the album x 5.21¢ (75% of the statutory rate), or (2)52.1¢ (10 x 5.21¢), depending on the contract.[35]

**If an artist uses songs from an outside songwriter (i.e., a non-controlled composition) and the outside songwriter insists on getting the full statutory amount (6.95¢), then the artist is very likely to end up receiving less than 75% of 6.95¢ on the songs the artist has written. The artist will receive, as income earned in his or her capacity as a songwriter, only what is left over from the mechanical royalty "pie" allotted for all of the songs written for the entire album. If a typical controlled composition clause is included as part of the record contract, mechanical royalties paid by the record company in excess of 52.1¢ per album will be charged as an advance against the artist's other royalties. This is complicated but important to know, because if an artist puts a song from an outside songwriter on the album, it can hurt the artist financially. And, if the artist does not think putting the outside songwriter's song on the album will make the artist more money than if the song was not on the album, the song won't be there.**

---

[35] Also, the record company will insist that no mechanical royalties on controlled compositions be paid on "free goods."

Here's an example: Suppose an artist's deal with the record company states that mechanical royalties paid in excess of 52.1¢ per album will be charged as an advance against the artist's other royalties. Also, for purposes of this example, assume that there are 12 songs on the album — 6 written by the artist, and 6 written by an outside songwriter who insists on receiving the full statutory mechanical royalty rate of 6.95¢.

| | |
|---|---:|
| Six outside songwriter songs (6.95¢ x 6) | 41.7¢ |
| Six songs written by artist (75% x 6.95¢ x 6) | + 31.3¢ |
| Total mechanical royalties payable by record company per album | 73.0¢ |
| Less: Per album mechanical pie (as agreed to in the artist's record contract) | − 52.1¢ |
| Amount payable in excess of album mechanical pie (charged as an advance against artist's other royalties) | = 20.9¢ |
| Net amount per album artist will actually receive for writing six songs on the album (31.3¢ minus 20.9¢) | 10.4¢ |

As you can see, the business reality of the controlled composition clause often forces all but the most sought after outside songwriters to accept a reduced mechanical royalty rate equal to 5.21¢ per song. Even sought after songwriters often accept a reduced mechanical royalty rate of 5.21¢ for sales of mid-line or budget records.[36]

---

[36] Canada has its own rates that are currently being reworked, but are generally economically tied to the U.S. rates. Except for the U.S. and Canada, most countries have entirely different copyright royalty systems. "Mechanicals" in these other countries are a set percentage of the retail price of the record.

# 2) PERFORMING ROYALTIES

**In exchange for the right to play songs in public, television stations, radio stations, night clubs and other public users of music pay <u>performing royalties</u>.**

Every nightclub, restaurant and other place you hear music publicly is charged a fee. (Yes, fees are even paid to play elevator music!) Since it would be too cumbersome for every public user of music to enter into a separate royalty agreement with each copyright owner of music, non-profit <u>performance rights societies</u> that represent the interests of songwriters and their publishers have come into existence.[37]

Songwriters and their publishers affiliate independently with a performance rights society.[38] In the U.S., <u>ASCAP</u> and <u>BMI</u> are the dominant performance rights societies.[39] Other countries have their equivalent societies.

For each public user of music, each society negotiates a separate licensing agreement. Most of the licensing agreements allow the public user to use all of the songs of all the copyright owners the society represents for a negotiated set fee (this is referred to as a <u>blanket license</u>).

---

[37] For political reasons, performance rights societies do not collect royalties for music performed in films playing in U.S. theaters.

[38] As a songwriter, you can be affiliated with only one society at any given time, and generally, your application will not be accepted by a society unless you have a song on a record that is, or will soon be, sold publicly. If a songwriter acts as his or her own publisher, a separate affiliation in their capacity as publisher is required.

[39] <u>SESAC</u> is the other performance rights society in the United States. It, however, controls less than 2% of U.S. performing rights. For clarity, we have limited our discussion to ASCAP and BMI, but the information given also applies to SESAC.

The society collects the "performing" royalties from each public user, deducts the society's expenses (currently about 20% of the money collected), and distributes the remainder to its songwriter and publisher members. Of the amount distributed, the songwriter members receive 50% and the publisher members receive 50%. Unlike the record companies who pay mechanical royalties to a publisher, who in turn pays the songwriter his or her agreed share, the performance rights societies pay affiliated songwriter members 50% directly (in addition to paying the publisher members 50% directly). As an individual songwriter, depending on your deal with your publisher, you may be entitled to part of your publisher's share of performing royalties, but these royalties will need to be collected from the publisher directly, not from the performance rights society.

## Allocation Of Royalty License Proceeds Among The Society's Members

Both ASCAP and BMI pay songwriter members and publisher members quarterly (i.e., four times a year). Payment occurs within six to nine months after the end of the three month period in which the performing monies were earned. Generally, even though every public user of music is charged a license fee, both ASCAP and BMI calculate payment to their members based on complicated formulas that rely solely on a song's radio and television airplay. Also, these societies use very different methods of calculating which songs and which songwriter members are entitled to what percentage of the income that will ultimately be distributed to the various songwriters.[40] Because

---

40 The most useful description we've seen of the various factors and formulas that determine the actual payment to songwriters, besides talking directly to ASCAP and BMI, is found in the book entitled, *Music, Money, and Success*, listed in the Recommended Reading section.

each songwriter's situation is unique, it is difficult to say which society pays its songwriters more in any given year. Once it becomes generally known that one society is paying a bit more than the other, the payments tend to equalize. Therefore, which society will ultimately be more beneficial to a new songwriter cannot be said with any degree of certainty.

To give you a rough idea of the dollars involved, a fairly popular BMI song generates 12¢ of income per play if played on a major radio station, and 6¢ per play if played on a lesser radio station. ASCAP's formulas defy calculation in this simple manner, but payments seem to equalize anyway.

If a song reaches number 1 on *Billboard's* "Hot 100," it is likely to be played publicly enough times in the first year of release to generate $250,000 to $500,000 in performing royalties (50% of this amount will be paid directly to the songwriter member(s) who wrote the song, and 50% will be paid to the publisher member(s) who published the song).

If a song only reaches number 20, it is likely to be played publicly enough times to generate $60,000 to $120,000 in performing royalties. If it tops out at number 100, it is likely to be played publicly only enough times to generate $4,000 to $6,000 in performing royalties.

As mentioned earlier a songwriter may be entitled to part of his or her publisher's share of performing royalties, but these royalties will need to be collected from the publisher directly, not from the performance rights society.

# 13. SECONDARY SOURCES OF INCOME

## FOREIGN MECHANICAL RIGHTS

Foreign royalties are becoming a larger percentage of the songwriter's profit picture as sales of U.S. artists' records boom internationally.

Most countries have mechanical rights collections organizations that license all musical compositions. Unlike the U.S., where mechanical licenses are based on a statutory rate per song, the mechanical amount collected in most foreign countries is based on a percentage of the retail price of a record. Foreign publishers are generally used to collect royalty monies earned in other countries because they are more aware of the nuances particular to a local country. Foreign publishers acting in this capacity are referred to as "sub-publishers" because they are accountable in the performance of their duties to the U.S. publisher.

## FOREIGN PERFORMING RIGHTS

Most every country has its own equivalent of ASCAP and BMI. ASCAP and BMI enter into contracts with these societies to collect monies for ASCAP and BMI songwriters. Approximately 1/4 of all performing monies received by ASCAP and BMI come from foreign societies, and this amount is growing rapidly.

Generally, publishers contract with foreign sub-publishers to collect the publisher's share of foreign performing royalties from each country's performing rights society because payment is much quicker than if the publisher contracted with the foreign performing rights societies directly. In a typical sub-publisher deal, the sub-publisher keeps 15% to 25% of the monies earned.

## SYNCHRONIZATION LICENSE FEES

In exchange for a fee, a synchronization ("sync") license is issued to companies producing television shows, movies and home videos that wish to synchronize a songwriter's music to their visual images. But remember, a songwriter does not have to license the use of his or her songs for television or film. There is no compulsory requirement to do so. That is why these fees are very fluid and depend on who needs who.

As an example, for national television commercials, a well-known song can earn as much as $300,000 for a one-year use in a major ad campaign ($50,000 to $150,000 is more the norm). The same song will earn $20,000 to $70,000 if used as the theme song of a major film; up to $50,000 if used somewhere in a film but not as the theme song; and typically less than $1,200 if used on television.

The sync fees for television are lower than those for film because (1)television budgets are lower, (2)television reaches a much wider audience and therefore reaches more potential record buyers, and (3)a song used on television will generate extra performing royalties.

## SHEET MUSIC

The royalty paid by a sheet music company is typically 20% of the retail selling price for sheet music containing a single song. Today, this equals 70¢ (20% of $3.50 — the typical retail price of sheet music). For historical reasons, if a songwriter has a contract with a major publishing house, the publishing house usually pays the songwriter only 5¢ to 15¢ of the 70¢.[41] Since the dollars involved are not large, this point is not often raised in the negotiations between publishing houses and songwriters.

"Folios" are collections of songs. The total royalty paid by sheet music companies for the songs included in a folio ranges from 10% to 12-1/2% of the retail selling price of the folio. Folios can be "mixed," "matching" or "personality" folios. A "mixed folio" is a collection of well-known songs made popular by various artists. A "matching folio" is a collection of songs from a particular album. "Personality folios" are those that have the artist's picture on the cover. In personality folios, an added 5% royalty is typically paid to the artist (for the use of the artist's name and likeness). Instructional print music (e.g., "How to play the piano" folios) bears a 10% royalty payment.[42]

---

[41] Major publishing companies customarily receive 10% to 12-1/2% of the retail selling price on sheet music sold outside of the U.S. and Canada, 50% of which typically goes to the songwriter.

[42] There are only four major manufactures of secular printed music in the U.S.: Warner/Chappell, Columbia Pictures Publishing, Hal Leonard and Cherry Lane.

# 14. MUSIC PUBLISHING

## PUBLISHERS

If you are like most artists and songwriters, you probably wonder what exactly publishers do and why so many people who have never made money in the music business tell you to "hang on to your publishing."

There is a lot more to publishing than filling out copyright registration forms and ASCAP/BMI forms. Full-service publishing companies find artists, record companies, film companies, television production companies, advertisers, etc. to use a songwriter's song. They negotiate licenses with anyone using the song and ensure that proper royalties are paid. They also monitor the song's public usage to make sure it is properly reported to the performance rights society, so that performing royalties are not lost. In short, a good full-service publisher generates more income from a song than the songwriter could, and the songwriter's time is freed up to write new songs.

Typically, in exchange for doing all of the above for the songwriter, a publisher insists that the songwriter transfer all of his or her official copyright "rights" (i.e., the rights of the copyright owner) to the publisher. The publisher and the songwriter then split the profits generated by the song. Review the "Your Copyright Monopoly" section of Chapter 10 for a refresher on the rights transferred.

Historically, the publisher received 50% of the song's profits. Over time, as the record industry has matured, the role of publishers is not as important as it once was. Many artists now write their own songs and act as their own publishers. Other

well-known songwriters do not need someone to find a recording artist for them; to the contrary, the artists seek <u>them</u> out. So
today, for successful songwriters with an established track record,
major publishing companies are, in essence, little more than fi-
nancing companies, advancing the songwriters money in exchange for anticipated profits from a song. The songwriter receives a steady income, and the publisher and songwriter agree
to "split the publishing" share of the income.

If, for example, the songwriter and publishing company
agree to "split the publishing" 50/50, then the songwriter retains
75% of the profits earned from the song (100% of the songwriter's share of profits, and 50% of the publisher's share of profits).

Nevertheless, through quirks of history, the holder(s) of the
<u>publisher's share</u> (regardless of who owns the "publishing" — i.e.,
the copyright rights) are generally said to receive 50% of the
song's profits. The remaining 50% is said to be the <u>writer's share</u>.
This is why the songwriter receives 50% of the performing royalties (i.e., the writer's share) directly from ASCAP or BMI.
Even if the songwriter has a contract with a publishing company that states that the songwriter is retaining an interest in the
publisher's share, the full publisher's share of performing royalties is generally paid by ASCAP or BMI directly to the major
publishing company.[43] It is up to the songwriter to make sure
that the publishing company pays the songwriter his or her portion of the retained publisher's share.

---

[43] ASCAP and BMI will not typically pay directly a publishing company which is
created by the writer in order to share the "publishing" with a major publishing company.

A major publishing company has many departments to ensure that the publisher's entire operation runs smoothly. The publisher's paperwork (e.g., registering songs with the copyright office, issuing licenses, making sure that the correct amount of royalties are being paid for the songs and disbursed to the writers) is handled by a combination of departments including what are often called the Business/Legal Affairs Department, the Copyright Department and the Royalties Department. Placing the publisher's songs with users, finding new songwriters, and improving the songwriter's songs so that the publisher has new songs to sell, are all handled by what is typically called the Creative Department.

EMI and Warner/Chappell are the biggest music publishers. These two companies own the rights to, and have to keep track of, literally tens of thousands of songs. Every time you hear the song "Happy Birthday" in a movie or on television, Warner/Chappell makes money. (Wouldn't you love to own the rights to that song?)

BMG, Famous, Irving/Almo, Jobete and MCA are also industry heavyweights, but because becoming a publishing company is not as financially difficult as becoming a record company, the publishing industry is not dominated by publishing companies the way the record industry is dominated by the "majors."

Essentially, there are only two key parts to a publishing company:

**Administrative** — to take care of the paperwork.
**Creative** — to find the writers, improve their songs and to run around schmoozing people in order to get songs recorded or used in movies and television.

That is why a publishing company does not have to be big to be successful. A song on a record label that lacks sufficient market presence and financial backing will not be widely heard, no matter how great the song is. A publishing company does not require the financial backing that a record company does. A publisher need only enter into a mechanical licensing agreement with a record company to place a song on an album. The marketing and promotion of the album will be financially supported by the record company.

You may have heard of the Harry Fox Agency. The Harry Fox Agency is a part of the National Music Publishers Association, which issues mechanical licenses for most publishers in the U.S., ensures that mechanical royalties are paid, and accounts to the publishers. They also perform occasional audits of the record companies to make sure that the right amount of mechanical royalties are being paid. For this service, the Harry Fox Agency charges 4-1/2% of the gross monies collected. In addition, for some publishers, the Harry Fox agency also issues sync licenses to film companies for use in movies for a fee of 10% of the gross monies collected. They also issue sync licenses to television production companies for a fee of 5% of the gross monies collected.

## SONGWRITER DEALS WITH PUBLISHERS

**When you are entering into a contract to give up part of your publishing, make sure that the publisher is providing you with a service that you anticipate will generate more money to you than you would otherwise receive if you did not do the deal. If you do not believe that a particular publisher will make you money, do not enter into the contract!**

There may be any number of reasons to have someone else handle your publishing. You may not want to do your own "administration." (It's a pain to do.) You may not have the contacts to get your song(s) to artists and other users of music. Or you may not be able to get an independent label to take you on as an artist unless you offset some of their risk by including some of your publishing. All of these reasons are valid. The important thing is to know why you are entering into the deal and to make sure that whoever you deal with makes you more money than you would otherwise make.[44]

A deal may be for a single song, where a songwriter and publisher agree to enter into a deal covering only one of the songwriter's songs. Another type of deal binds the songwriter as an exclusive songwriter for the publishing company for a specific period of time. This means that the publishing company will be the publisher of every song the songwriter writes during the term of their agreement. A variation of the exclusive songwriter deal is a writer-artist development deal, where the publisher is actively trying to land a record deal for the songwriter who is also an artist. If the publisher is successful in getting a record deal for the songwriter/artist, presumably many of songwriter/publisher-owned songs will be on the album.

Often, songwriters receive advances from a full-service publishing company on the anticipated income stream their songs are expected to generate. If the songwriter is an exclusive

---

[44] Along the same lines, do not be surprised if an artist who "picks up" your song changes a few of the words and asks to be included as a songwriter on the song. Remember, it is about money. If you need the artist more than the artist needs your song, it may be worth including the artist as one of the songwriters of the song. A co-writer of one song on a Madonna album makes much more than a writer of many songs that appear on an album of a lesser-known artist.

songwriter for the publishing company, this provides the songwriter with a steady income that frees the songwriter from monthly economic worry. As part of this type of deal with a full-service publishing company, a new songwriter may be expected to give up all of his or her interest in the publisher's share (i.e., 50% of the gross dollars earned). This, however, may not be necessary if the publisher believes in your songs and you are willing to take smaller advances against anticipated income from royalties. Advances for new songwriters rarely exceed $3,500 per month. In the current climate, unless the songwriter already has an "in" with major recording artists, or the songwriter is an aspiring artist for whom the major publishing company believes it can land a record deal, a major publishing company is not likely to sign a songwriter.

There are many nuances that define the various deals a songwriter may enter into with a publisher. Songwriters often enter into what are referred to as "co-publishing" deals and "administrative" deals. These terms mean different things to different people in the industry, and what they mean must be spelled out in each contract.

A "co-publishing" deal is entered into by a songwriter and a publisher when the songwriter and publisher agree to share the publishing. This type of deal is often entered into when the songwriter's songs are expected to generate a lot of income for the publishing company, and the songwriter has his or her own outlets for the songs. Typically, in deals such as this, the publisher's share of income is split 50/50. This means that the songwriter retains 75% of the songs' earning power (i.e., 100% of the songwriter's share and 50% of the publisher's share).

If an "administration deal" is entered into by a songwriter and a publisher, there will be no advances, and the publishing company will limit its role to administrative tasks. Copyright ownership of the songs may be retained by a separate publishing entity controlled by the songwriter, the term of the agreement may be shorter, and a lesser percentage of publishing (i.e., the publisher's share) will be given to the administrative publishing company. Typically, the administrative publisher receives 7-1/2% to 20% of the gross dollars earned in such deals. The more income a songwriter's songs have generated in previous years, the lower the publisher's percentage. Also, the specific services rendered play a part in determining the percentage earned by the publishing company. For instance, Bug International, a publishing company that specializes in administrative deals and typically charges 15%, does help songwriters find users for their songs, a function considered "creative."

# 15. KEY PUBLISHING CONTRACT DEAL POINTS

As with the key record contract deal points, the key points discussed below, to one extent or another, deal with whether money ends up in the songwriter's pocket or in the publisher's pocket. (Remember, a songwriter may own part of his or her own publishing too.)

Keep this list as a handy reference tool when you are negotiating or renegotiating your publishing deal. Insist that your lawyer explain each item to you in detail.

## 1) TERM

The term of an exclusive songwriter deal with a major publisher will usually be for one year, and gives the publisher the right to exercise several consecutive one-year options. Try to limit the number of options to three or fewer. A writer-artist development deal may be for as long as two years. This allows the publisher more time to get the songwriter a record deal. If it is successful, the publishing house will generally insist on having an option to extend the publishing agreement for the life of the record deal.

## 2) RIGHTS TRANSFERRED / USE OF SONG(S)

The publisher will want all of the songwriter's rights transferred to it. There are some rights that you may not wish your publisher to exercise. You may wish to limit your publisher's right to do one or more of the following without your approval:

a. Change the title of the song.
b. Change the words or music.
c. Allow it to be synchronized to X-rated films.
d. Allow it to be synchronized to advertisements.
e. Translate the words into a foreign language.
f. Allow someone else to modify your song and share in the royalties from the derivative work.

Also, remember that <u>compulsory</u> mechanical licenses need not be issued until after the first public use of the song. A songwriter who is also an artist may want to deny the publisher the right to issue a negotiated license to anyone other than the songwriter until after the songwriter's song has appeared on his or her own album.

Finally, the publisher may ask the songwriter to transfer all rights to all of the songwriter's material written prior to the date the agreement was entered into. If this is the case, make sure that you are being compensated for these additional songs.

## 3) ROYALTIES

Major publishing companies are often owned by a parent company that owns a major record and/or film company. Make sure that the publisher cannot issue mechanical licenses at less than customary rates to its affiliated companies. Do this even if you are entitled to receive part of the "publisher's share."

Your contract with the publisher should call for "the songwriter" to receive 50% of <u>all</u> monies collected (except performing rights monies paid directly to the songwriter from ASCAP or BMI).

# 4) ADVANCES

If a songwriter signs an agreement with a major publishing company allowing his or her songs to be published by the publishing company, the publishing company may agree to pay the songwriter advances on its anticipated profits from the songwriter's songs. The bigger the percentage of profits given up by the songwriter, the higher the advance should be. The amount of the advance is based on how much money the publishing company expects to make from the songs. The range is from $0 to a high percentage of the money earned by the songwriter's songs in the previous year(s). Of course, the advances will be recoupable from royalties when actually received by the publishing company from licensees.

Often, the publisher negotiates to receive advances from third parties to whom they license the songs. For instance, a record company may give the publishing company an advance against anticipated mechanical royalties the publishing company and songwriter will earn from a record that is going to be released. The agreement between the songwriter and publisher should include a provision entitling the songwriter to participate in all advances paid to the publisher by third parties for licenses.

# 5) RESERVE LIMITATIONS

Usually, publishers are paid by record companies quarterly, and "reserves" of 50% to 75% are retained by the record company. These reserves are often held for as long as two years. Since the record company does not have any cross-collateralization rights against the publisher, the reserve the record company withholds from the publisher is much larger than the reserve the record company withholds from the artist's royalty. So, just because you have a song on a major album, don't expect to see any money immediately.

Even though record companies pay the publisher quarterly, publishers typically try to pay the songwriter only twice a year. Every effort should be made to get your publisher to pay you quarterly.

## 6) COPYRIGHT OWNERSHIP REVERSION

Generally, the rights to your song(s) are sold to the publisher for the life of the copyright in exchange for your participation in royalty payments.[45] You should try to negotiate for reversion of the copyright if certain criteria are not met by the publisher (e.g., placing a song on a record within a certain time period).

## 7) WORK FOR HIRE

Remember, the copyright of a "work for hire" is owned from the outset by the person or entity doing the hiring, not the actual songwriter. Make sure that your publishing contract specifically states that your songs are not works for hire and are not written within the scope of employment by the publisher. Even if a publisher offers to pay you your share of royalties in exchange for making your songs works for hire, it is not in your best interest to do so. If one of your songs becomes a standard, it will

---

[45] If the original owner of a copyrighted work created after January 1, 1978 sends timely notice to the publisher, the publishing rights revert back to the original owner after 35 years. (The notice can be sent as early as 10 years before the effective date of the reversion.) The additional 19 years for older copyrighted works also revert back to the original copyright owner upon giving effective notice.

have value for many years. One of the quirks in the copyright law allows the original owner of a song to reclaim full copyright ownership after 35 years.[46] If you are not the original owner, you will not be entitled to exercise this right of copyright reversion.[47]

## 8) MINIMUM SONG DELIVERY

In most publishing contracts, especially those in which a publishing company is paying the songwriter an advance, a minimum song delivery requirement is added to ensure that the songwriter is actually working. Typically, this averages about twelve songs per year (one per month). In a situation where you write a song with someone else (i.e., collaborations), you will only receive credit for having written half of a song.

## 9) COLLABORATIONS

Make sure that there are no prohibitions against collaborating with songwriters who have other publishers. You should only be responsible for transferring your share of ownership of the collaborated song to the publisher.

## 10) EXCEPTIONS TO EXCLUSIVITY

Even though a songwriter's agreement may be exclusive, there may be certain situations that you wish to exclude from your agreement with the publisher. For instance, if you are writ-

---

[46] See footnote 45.

[47] Never allow your song to be referred to in any contract as a "work for hire," unless you are being paid considerable money for a particular project (e.g., to work on a film).

ing a song specifically for a film, oftentimes the film company will insist on receiving the copyright and you may need this flexibility.

Also, for contracts with publishers in California, be aware of Civil Code §3423(e) and Code of Civil Procedure §526(5), both of which deal with personal service contracts. Essentially, these code provisions deny a publisher the right to obtain an injunction to stop you from writing for someone else (even if you agreed to provide the publisher your exclusive services), unless the publisher pays you a minimum compensation of $9,000 in the first year, $12,000 in the second year, and substantially more in years three through seven.

## 11) CO-PUBLISHING ISSUES

A "co-publishing deal" is entered into not only when a songwriter keeps part of his or her publishing, but also if two "real" publishing companies are publishers of a song (e.g., when each songwriter that collaborates on a song has a different publisher).

If there is a co-publishing deal, two major issues arise apart from "official" ownership of the copyright. The first issue is who is entitled to "administer" the song (and gets paid to do so). It is always better to have you or your publisher keep the administration.

The other major issue is determining what monies get divided among the various publishers. This amount can be disputed because each publisher may be performing different functions and incurring different costs in doing so.

## 12) INFRINGEMENT CLAIMS

We live in a lawsuit-happy society. Anyone can claim that you infringed on their song and start a costly legal battle. A publishing company will generally insist on (1)being indemnified by you for the full costs of the lawsuit, (2)retaining control over the litigation, and (3)holding as a "reserve" (instead of paying you) the money that is being sued for, regardless of whether the lawsuit is justified or not. At the very least, a songwriter should insist that if the lawsuit is unsuccessful, the publisher will pay for its share of the legal fees.

## 13) LIMITS ON FOREIGN SUB-PUBLISHER FEES

Most publishers use foreign sub-publishers to collect royalties from other countries because of the nuances particular to each country. If the agreement between the songwriter and publisher states that the songwriter and publisher are to split the net foreign royalties received by the publisher (after the sub-publisher takes its fees), then the songwriter, at least to some extent, is really paying for publishing twice. A songwriter should try to receive royalties "at the source." This means that the songwriter will share royalties 50/50 <u>before</u> the sub-publisher's share is deducted.

## 14) ACCOUNTINGS AND AUDITING RIGHTS

You should be sure your contract requires periodic accountings from the publishing company that detail (1)payments received from record companies, (2)other licensing fees received by the publisher for use of your songs, (3)payments from sub-publishers, and (4)expenses charged to your account. Also, insist that the contract allow you to conduct a detailed audit of the publisher's books. The more rights you have, the better. This can help prevent the publishing company from becoming sloppy with your account.

# 16. CREATING YOUR OWN PUBLISHING COMPANY

Here is a basic guide to creating your own publishing company:

1. If you are a songwriter and are setting up your own publishing company, before you do anything else, first apply for affiliation with a performance rights society. The reason to do this is because if the name of your company is similar to others, ASCAP/BMI will turn the application down (i.e., they will not collect money for you). It is therefore smart to apply before your company has spent money on promotional material.

You must apply separately as a songwriter and as a publisher to the same performance rights society (i.e., apply to either ASCAP as both a songwriter and publisher or apply to BMI as both a songwriter and publisher). If your intention is to become a publishing company for other songwriters as well, separate applications as a publisher to both ASCAP and BMI should be made, and two different publishing company names must be chosen and used. It can take over a month to get approved.

ASCAP and BMI will provide you with lists of names currently being used by publishing companies affiliated with them. BMI will even reserve a company name for you (upon request and for a limited time only) if it is not being used by another publisher.

You can contact ASCAP and BMI as follows:

**ASCAP**: 1 Lincoln Plaza, New York, NY 10023; tel. (212) 621-6000; fax (212) 724-9064; and at 7920 Sunset Blvd, Suite 300, Los Angeles, CA 90046; tel. (213) 883-1000; fax (213) 883-1049.

**BMI**: 320 West 57th Street, New York, NY 10019; tel. (212) 586-200; fax (212) 489-2368; and at 8730 Sunset Blvd, 3rd Floor, Hollywood, CA 90069; tel. (310) 659-9109; fax (310) 657-6947.

2. If your company is not a corporation using its corporate name, in most states it must file a document with the county recorder in which the publishing company is located stating, among other things, the business name that you are operating under. The exact name of the document and the specific requirements vary from state to state, but your county recorder should be able to guide you through your state's particular maze.

In California, the document is called the Fictitious Business Name Statement ("FBNS"). The FBNS must not only be filed with the county recorder's office, but must also appear in a newspaper of general circulation. Your county recorder can tell you which newspapers are acceptable and, based on circulation, which is probably the least expensive.

3. Register the songs with the Copyright Office in Washington, D.C. in the name of your publishing entity. If you have previously registered the songs, file an assignment transferring the copyright ownership of the songs to the publishing entity.

Well, it's time for a break. The following pages contain **THE "BIG PICTURE" ROYALTY CHART** which summarizes the largest royalty payments to artists and songwriters.

# THE "BIG PICTURE"

## ARTIST'S LARGEST ROYALTIES

### Record Royalties:

**From record sales.** Paid by the record company to the artist in exchange for allowing the record company to make a record featuring the artist.

The amount paid is typically a percentage of the suggested retail list price (SRLP) of the record, less many deductions.

### Other Royalties:

**From film/TV sync license fees.** Paid by film companies, television production companies and many others to the record company for the right to use the record company's master recording of the artist's version of the song.

The record company pays the artist his or her share of the fees as agreed to in the record contract.

# ROYALTY CHART

## SONGWRITER'S LARGEST ROYALTIES

### Mechanical Royalties:

**From record sales.** Paid by a record company to the publisher for the right to include the songwriter's song on a record. The publisher pays the songwriter his or her share.

The publisher receives 100% of this royalty, which is divided into two equal parts (50/50) called (1)the writer's share, and (2)the publisher's share.

The publisher pays the songwriter the entire writer's share.

The publisher pays the songwriter any part of the publisher's share retained by the songwriter in the agreement between the songwriter and publisher.

### Performing Royalties:

**From airplay.** Paid by broadcasters such as radio stations, television stations and other public performance users of a song.

This royalty is divided into two equal parts (50/50) called (1)the writer's share, and (2)the publisher's share. Monies are paid to ASCAP / BMI / SESAC .

These so-called "performance rights societies" pay the songwriter directly the entire writer's share. The society pays the publisher the publisher's share. If part of the publisher's share is retained by the songwriter, the publisher pays the songwriter that part of the publisher's share.

### Other Royalties:

**From sheet music sales, and film/TV sync license fees.** Paid by sheet music companies, film companies, television production companies and many others to the publisher for the right to use a song.

The publisher receives 100% of this royalty from the use of the song and, in turn, pays the songwriter his or her share in the same manner that mechanical royalties are paid to the songwriter.

# OTHER IMPORTANT BASICS

## 17. ISSUES BETWEEN BAND MEMBERS

**This is one of the least favorite things for band members to discuss. When you are just starting out, everything is great because it's all about the music. Issues between band members, however, must be discussed.**

Apart from enjoying the music, make sure that you really like being with the other members of your band. If you are successful, you will be touring together, promoting your band together, and generally spending lots and lots of time together.

Not only does spending a great deal of time with people you don't like become old very quickly, but like it or not, <u>you will also be in business with them</u>. Life is too short for the nightmares that follow when the inevitable disagreements about money surface. If you haven't "made it" yet, you won't think it's an issue, but it will be. When band members do not like each other, money fights can become very nasty.

When a band is just forming, you cannot anticipate or protect against all of the things that may happen, and until you truly believe that the band is going somewhere, it doesn't make sense to spend a lot of money on a lawyer. But once you believe the band <u>is</u> going to be together for a while, it makes sense to hire a lawyer and have him or her draw up an internal band contract.

A good contract between band members will address critical issues, including who owns the band's name in the event of a breakup, who gets what percentages of profits, and who controls the band's business decisions such as when to tour or firing other band members. If you are the "Pete Best" of the group (The Beatles' drummer before Ringo Starr), waiting until a record deal is at hand to raise these issues may be too late. It's better to find out early on where everybody stands.

If the band does <u>not</u> have a written contract, the band is treated as a legal partnership. And like a partnership, when one of the band members (i.e., one of the partners) leaves the band, for whatever reason, then legally that partnership terminates automatically.

Of course, the remaining members of the band are free to form a new band, but legally they may not be free to use the old band's name without paying the departing member for the privilege of doing so. This is because without a written contract, the law generally presumes that each band member owns an equal share of the band's physical assets (e.g., the equipment) <u>and</u> intangible assets (e.g., the band's name and logo). Each member of the band is also presumed to (1) share equally in the band's profits and losses, and (2) have an equal vote in the band's affairs. Majority rules!

Quite apart from issues centering around the band's formation and demise are terms of the band's record deal itself, which may leave a band member's ego bruised. Provisions in record contracts must be spelled out. Is the record company going to treat one member as more valuable than the rest? If one member refuses to record, are all the members in breach of the contract? If one member leaves the group, does the record company have the right to void the record deal? Who is responsible to the record company if the band is still "in the red" when one member leaves the band?

A good contract between band members will address the rights and obligations of each individual member. Work out the details with your attorney before you get too big or you may be in for some nasty legal fights down the road.

# 18. TRADEMARKS AND SERVICE MARKS

Your name and logo as a band are potentially valuable assets. You can cripple your future earning power before your career even begins if you don't have an identity that is your own and can't be used by others. Had "The Beatles" spelled the band name "The Beetles," they would have lost millions in royalties because the name of a bug, spelled correctly, would have legally offered them little identity protection.

Often, people use the term "copyright" when they really mean "trademark" or "service mark." Basically, the difference is that copyrights protect the *expression* of artistic ideas (e.g., a songwriter's songs), and trademarks/service marks protect the *identifying symbols* associated with a particular product or service.[48]

More specifically, a <u>trademark</u> is a brand name or logo used to identify physical goods, while a <u>service mark</u> is a brand name or logo used to identify services. A band's name is used as a brand name to identify services offered (i.e., your music), and therefore, the appropriate mark is a service mark. But if you are using the band's name on T-shirts or other forms of merchandise, you are offering physical goods for sale and the appropriate mark is a trademark.

**In the United States, the rights to use a particular band name are generally based on which band uses the name first.**

---

48 Copyrights are discussed more fully in Chapter 10.

**The name is not owned by the person who thought it up, but rather by who <u>uses</u> it (i.e., the band).** Even though the rights are created by use, and not by registration with either the U.S. Patent and Trademark Office or the individual state's Secretary of State, it is a good idea when you start becoming successful to register the name of your band with the U. S. Patent and Trademark Office. By doing so, if anyone does infringe on your mark, you will be in a better position to recover damages from them.

The symbols TM and SM are unofficial and are used only to give notice to others that you claim trademark TM or service mark SM ownership for an unregistered mark. Use them liberally. You can only place the symbol ® at the end of your band's name if you have obtained a federally registered mark.

Before registering, here are a few tips:

Make the name of your band original. When you hit it big, you don't want someone suing you because they were using the name before you were. Even if another band was first to use a name that is not the same as yours but that the public would confuse with your name, the U. S. Patent and Trademark Office will not issue you a trademark or service mark.

The best way to ensure that your name is original is to hire a professional search bureau to search the records of the U. S. Patent and Trademark Office and those of all fifty states. This will cost several hundred dollars.

If you cannot afford to hire a professional search firm (such as those listed in your local yellow pages under "trademark consultants"), at least check trade sources such as: (1)the American Federation of Musicians (AFM),[49] whose offices will tell you whether they have an exclusive agency contract with a group that already is using the name you want; (2)*Pollstar, Billboard's International Talent & Touring Directory* or *The Yellow Pages of Rock*, which list most of the groups that are actively performing; and (3)record stores.

The address and telephone number for the U.S. Patent and Trademark Office in Washington is: U.S. Department of Commerce/Patent and Trademark Office, Washington, D.C. 20231; tel. (703) 308-4357. When an application to register a mark is made, the U.S. Patent and Trademark Office first looks for other marks that may be the same as, or similar to, yours. Then they publish your proposed mark in the *U.S. Official Gazette* so that others can look at your mark and raise objections, if they have any. It takes roughly nine months to a year to obtain the registration if everything goes perfectly and no one has any objection to the registration of your mark.

The minimum registration fee itself is $245, but proper registration of a mark can cost much more. This fee does not include your attorneys' fees, which will be a minimum of several hundred dollars assuming everything goes smoothly.

We do not suggest trying to register your mark without enlisting the help of an attorney, since there are many technicalities and many things that can go wrong. Also, there are follow-up forms and renewal forms that must be completed to ensure that the mark stays yours for a long time.

---

[49] The American Federation of Musicians has offices at 1501 Broadway, Suite 600, New York, NY 10036; tel. (212) 869-1330; and at 1777 North Vine Street, Suite 500, Hollywood, CA 90028; tel. (213) 461-3441.

# 19. ON TOUR

The major touring season is May through September, but no one except major stars makes any real money touring. For everyone else, touring is done to help promote record sales.

The contracts used for tours booked by music agents are customarily AFM standard printed forms. The real "guts" of such tour agreements, however, are attached to the form. The attachment is called a <u>rider</u> to the contract, and it can be over 25 pages long. Important items of negotiation include limiting promoter expenses, merchandising, and technical specifications such as an artist's equipment, lighting and stage setup requirements.

If, for any reason, you (as an artist or a band) are booking your own tours, always make sure you have a written contract signed by the club owner <u>before</u> you show up to perform at a club. Many times the dates of performance, compensation, and the sound equipment to be provided get screwed up if an artist does not have a written contract.

New artists should not tour until their record is out. If you just made your own CD and are getting only a little airplay on college radio, don't expect any club to pay you more than $200 a night. More than likely, they will give you a percentage of the gross proceeds from ticket sales. The percentage may be as high as 65% or so, but may be a lot lower if other artists are playing there that night as well.

If an artist's record is beginning to sell well, the artist can get paid $250 to $2,000 a night from either headlining at a club or by opening for a major act. Oftentimes, however, the contract still calls for the artist to receive a percentage of the gross proceeds from ticket sales. If an artist does five shows a week ($2,000 x 5), the artist may gross $10,000 a week. However, it is more likely to be less. Even so, this may sound like pretty good money until you compare the gross income to the expense of going on tour.

It can *easily* cost $10,000 or more to "economically" put a band on the road for a week without the members drawing any salary (you must pay for food and lodging, equipment rental, truck or bus rental, a minimal crew, insurance, and commissions to agents and managers). An artist or a band can lose a lot of money by going on tour! Sometimes, money may be advanced by the record company as "tour support" because the record company wants the artist out there selling records.

A moderately successful artist (i.e., 200,000 to 500,000 album sales) may be able to break even on tours. He or she can headline in 2000-seat venues and get paid $5,000 or more per night, but the primary purpose of the tour is still to sell records.

Major stars make money on tours even though the costs can be astronomical. Michael Jackson took over 400 people with him on his last international tour! Major stars get paid minimum guarantees (up to $100,000 per night) against a percentage of net profits of the show (85% is typical; 90% if the artist is willing to forgo the guarantee). The promoter keeps the rest.

The amount of money made on tour seems to depend greatly on the type of music the artist performs. For instance, rock groups seem to draw much larger crowds than rap or hip-hop artists. Metallica does extremely well in concert. Mariah Carey sells a lot of albums, but does not draw a huge concert audience.

# 20. SELLING MERCHANDISE

Once you have your record deal and publishing deal in place, you will have plenty of advisors to protect you with regard to merchandising.

If you are just starting out, you are probably selling your own CDs, silk-screened T-shirts and caps at your shows. We do not mean to scare you (and as long as you are relatively small no one may care very much), but be aware that when you sell merchandise there are rules. There are city taxes, state taxes, business license fees and other local fees that must be paid. If you have a "roadie" or a friend doing the selling for you, they may technically be an "employee" of yours and payroll taxes must be paid. In any event, you probably won't be making a lot of money from merchandise sales until you hit the big time.

With rare exceptions, during a tour of a successful artist, the artist will license the right to use his or her name and likeness to a merchandiser. There are really only six major tour merchandisers, but there are a surprising number of bidding wars that serve to increase artist royalties. Winterland Productions, which is affiliated with the Bill Graham organization, and Brockum Merchandising are the largest. The other four are affiliated with major labels: Nice Man (BMG), Great Southern (PolyGram), Sony Signatures (Sony), and Giant (WEA). The royalty paid to the artist is generally 28% to 32% of the gross sales of the merchandise. Major stars can receive 40% or more of the gross, or 90% of the net profits. Generally, gross sales of merchandise of adult-oriented groups (e.g., Rod Stewart, Sting, etc.) can average $5 per person at the concert. Heavy metal groups can sell $8 of merchandise per person. Superstars, such as Michael Jackson or Madonna, may sell $12 of merchandise per person. The average sales per person do go down at larger venues.

Keep your image in mind. You don't want "schlock" out there with your name on it. Items of negotiation with a merchandising company include the amount of advances to the artist, creative control over the merchandise, the merchandiser's exclusive right to market, performance guarantees (i.e., that the artist or band will show up and play before a given number of people during the tour), and sell-off rights of excess merchandise at the end of the tour.

For merchandise sold at places other than concerts, the royalties paid by merchandisers to the artist for the right to manufacture the goods (or sub-license someone else to do so in the U.S.) are generally a lot less. One night of sales at a major concert can net the artist more than a full year of nationwide retail sales. Typically, royalties for clothing (mostly T-shirts and caps) sold at retail outlets are 10% to 12-1/2% of the retail sales price, while royalties for other items (such as bumper stickers, buttons and posters) are 8% to 10% of the sales price.

Mail-order companies pay roughly the same royalty percentages as the retail stores. However, some contracts with mail-order companies are arranged as "net" deals, with the artist receiving anywhere from 50% to 70% of "net" profits.

# 21. A LITTLE ABOUT MUSIC VIDEOS

Back in 1983, the trade magazine *Billboard* estimated that consistent exposure on MTV was boosting record sales by 15% to 20%. This started a boom. Now music videos are on television everywhere. Today, many music buyers find out about new music from television, not radio. Therefore, television's influence on the music scene is greater than ever.

Typically, the cost of making a professional video is $60,000 to $80,000 for a new or moderately successful artist, $100,000 to $200,000 or even higher for a major star. Unless you are signed to a label and have national distribution of your record in place, forget the idea of having MTV play your video.

You can, however, make a decent video for as low as $10,000 to $15,000 and have it played on local cable access, but in our experience it is generally not a good use of funds. If you feel you must make a video, here are a few budget-saving tips that have been passed on to us from video producers:

1. Use exterior daylight or minimal lighting.
2. Forget dance numbers.
3. Put your money into editing the video and synchronizing the music to it; rely on favors for rehearsals, getting the best video and sound equipment you can, and the video shoot itself.

# MUSIC, MOTION PICTURES & TELEVISION

This topic really requires a book of its own, and will probably not be too important to an artist or songwriter who is not already signed to a record or publishing deal, or is not a good friend of either a movie/television music coordinator or an executive with an advertising music supplier. Nevertheless, the following pages contain some highlights.

Remember, there is no compulsory license that allows film companies, television production companies and advertising agencies to use your song or your performance of a song without permission. Therefore, the fees are negotiable and highly volatile.

# 22. THEATRICAL MOTION PICTURES

In order to obtain the rights to use even one performance of a song as part of a motion picture, a film company may need to enter into many separate contracts. The film company may need to make deals with the performing artist, the songwriter (and publisher), the record company of the performer (both to use existing masters and clearing the right to use the record company's exclusive artist on the film soundtrack album), and finally, the record company that is going to make the film soundtrack album.

There are essentially three categories of music that may be part of a motion picture: (1)songs which are specifically written to be an integral part of a motion picture (e.g., "Can You Feel the Love Tonight" in the movie *The Lion King*); (2)songs which were not originally written for the film but are used in the film (e.g., "Hound Dog" in the movie *Forrest Gump*; and (3)the background music you hear throughout a film while actors are conversing and action is taking place (this is the movie's "score," also known as the "underscore").

## 1) SONGS SPECIFICALLY WRITTEN FOR A PARTICULAR MOTION PICTURE

Before the artist or songwriter can make a deal with the film company, both must make sure that they are allowed to do so under the terms of their record contract and publishing contract, respectively.[50]

## The Artist

For a song specifically written for a particular motion picture, the artist receives a flat fee (for the performance itself) and royalties (if a movie soundtrack album is made).[51] The amount of the fee can be all over the board and depends mostly on who needs who. A major artist may receive as much as $250,000 to $300,000 up front. A falling star in need of publicity, by contrast, may perform a song for as little as minimum union scale if the film is right. The total royalty paid on the soundtrack album (divided by all of the artists appearing on the album) is usually 10% to 12% of the SRLP. This percentage can, of course, be higher if one of the artists is a major star. Typically, an artist's record company will want to keep 50% of their artist's royalties (for letting the artist out of their "exclusive" arrangement) if the soundtrack album is released by another record company.

## The Songwriter

Typically, a songwriter is hired to write a song for a movie as a "work for hire." The songwriter's payment is a flat fee plus songwriter royalties. The fee can range anywhere from $0 to $35,000, depending on how established the songwriter is and how important the film company believes the song will be to the movie. Generally, however, film companies almost never obligate themselves to use a particular song, although with an established songwriter they will usually agree to pay for the song

---

[50] Major artists who write their own songs often negotiate "package deals" with film and television production companies, whereby the artist/songwriter receives one upfront fee and a combination of royalties which, in effect, merges the royalties earned from being both the artist and the songwriter.

[51] Royalty payments may also be earned from foreign distribution of the film.

whether they ultimately use it or not. Film companies also enter into "step" deals — where a film company pays the songwriter a small amount initially to make the demo, and then more later if the film company ultimately decides to use the song. Often, intermediate payments between the initial demo and ultimate completion of a song (i.e., "step" payments) are tied to refinements of the song made by the songwriter at the film company's request.

The songwriter's royalties are the same as those for any other ordinary songwriter deal.[52] If the songwriter is well-established, the songwriter may retain a portion of the "publisher's share" as well, but the film company usually retains ownership of the copyright and administration rights.

## 2) SONGS WHICH WERE NOT ORIGINALLY WRITTEN FOR A FILM BUT ARE LATER USED IN A FILM

For songs which were not originally written for a particular film but are later used in that film, the film company has to acquire a license from the artist's record company <u>and</u> the songwriter's publisher. Here is how the artist and songwriter get paid:

### The Artist

If the film company wants to use a particular version of a song that is already on a record, the film company must obtain a <u>master recording license</u> from the record company. This gives the film company the right to use the record company's master

---

[52] See Chapter 12, "Primary Sources of Income," Chapter 13, "Secondary Sources of Income," and Chapter 14, "Music Publishing."

recording. The artist typically receives 50% of the license royalty (i.e., whatever percentage is in the artist-record company contract). The license royalty fees charged by record companies can range from $10,000 to $50,000. If the deal calls for granting the film company rights to make a soundtrack album, the film company will pay an additional royalty of 10% to 12% of the SRLP. Typically, the artist's record company will retain half of these royalties and the artist will receive the other half.

## The Songwriter

To use the master recording, however, the film company must also negotiate with the copyright owner (i.e., the publisher) for a sync license, giving them the right to use the musical composition. Without the sync license, the song cannot be used and the master recording license obtained from the record company is worthless. Synchronization fees for publishing are often similar to those paid to the record company for use of the master recording ($10,000 to $50,000), although there seems to be a trend developing whereby more is being paid for the sync license.

## 3) THE BACKGROUND SCORE

For writing the score of a major film, the composer will receive a fee ranging from $30,000 to $150,000 (unless you are John Williams or Jerry Goldsmith, in which case the fee is closer to $500,000). In addition to songwriter royalties, the composer may also receive a royalty payment for each record sold (like artists) if the composer conducts the orchestra (5% to 9% of the SRLP) or produces the recordings (2% to 3% of the SRLP).

With the necessary use licenses in hand, the film company is free to strike a deal with any record/distribution company to put out a soundtrack album. Often, all three categories of music discussed above are a part of the same film and will be included in varying degrees on the soundtrack album. If only some of the music on a soundtrack album is expected to be the catalyst that generates the sales, the amount of royalties different people and entities are to receive from that soundtrack album will be heavily contested.

# 23. TELEVISION

The licenses that must be obtained for use of a song in television shows and made-for-TV movies are the same as those for theatrical motion pictures. There are some differences between the two mediums, however. First, unlike songs used in theatrical motion pictures shown in U.S. theaters, the songwriter will receive performing royalties (i.e., ASCAP/BMI payments) from songs used on television. Second, in part because payments are received from ASCAP/BMI, and in part because the exposure from television is much greater than that of film, payments to the artist and songwriter for songs used in television are much smaller. The exposure helps trigger an increase in the other sources of income from a song.

As with motion pictures, there are essentially three categories of music that may be part of a television program: (1) songs specifically written for a particular television program; (2) songs which were not originally written for a particular program but are later used in one; and (3) the television background score.

## 1) SONGS WRITTEN SPECIFICALLY FOR A PARTICULAR TELEVISION PROGRAM

There are not many songs written specifically for a particular television program other than the theme song. Since most television theme songs are composed by the show's background composers, these songs are often included as part of the initial background composing contract. This contract will generally state that all of the songs written by the composer for the television program are "works for hire."

## 2) SONGS WHICH WERE NOT ORIGINALLY WRITTEN FOR A PARTICULAR TELEVISION PROGRAM BUT ARE LATER USED IN ONE

With regard to the use of preexisting songs in a television show, the producer must secure the rights to use such songs from the publishers who own them. The standard sync fees charged by publishers range from $500 to $1,200 for a license authorizing use of a song in a television program or series for unlimited distribution for 3 to 5 years, but for hit shows such as *Frasier* and *Seinfeld,* the sync fee can be as high as $10,000. Usually, option rights to use the song beyond the five-year period and on re-runs is negotiated at the same time. If a well-known song is going to be used as the theme song for a television program, the publisher may charge the television production company anywhere from $1,500 to $10,000 per episode.

If the producer wishes to use a particular version of the song that is on a record, a separate master recording license must be obtained from the record company. This is like free advertising for future sales of the record company's record, and so the fees charged are low.

## 3) THE BACKGROUND SCORE

The background score constitutes the vast majority of the music heard on television. Such fees can range from $1,500 to $7,000 per episode ($8,000 to $25,000 for a package of multiple episodes), depending on such factors as how established the composer is, the length of the program being written for, and the size of the music budget. As with other music composed for movies and television, the standard television background composing contract states that the composer's music is a "work for hire." Therefore, the composer does not retain ownership of the copyright. The composer may, however, retain an interest in the royalties earned by the background score.

In a properly negotiated contract, when an American television program or made-for-TV movie is re-released in foreign movie theaters or on pay television in the U.S. (e.g., Cinemax, HBO), an additional fee equal to roughly 100% of the original fee will be paid to the artist and/or songwriter. Also, an additional fee equal to 50% to 75% of the original fee is paid if the television program or movie is distributed for home video use.

# 24. JINGLES

Jingles are songs used primarily for advertising on television and radio. In order to get your song used as a jingle, you will have to have an "in" with an advertising agency, an advertising music supplier (e.g., a "jingle house" representing many composers), or a producer producing such music. There are essentially two types of songs used as jingles: (1)songs written for a specific advertising campaign, and (2)existing songs.

## 1) SONGS WRITTEN FOR A SPECIFIC AD CAMPAIGN

After an advertising campaign is selected by a company and its ad agency, a music supplier is hired to provide the *music* for the jingle if the agency does not write the music in-house. The music supplier may be an independent writer or a jingle production company which is typically owned by a writer. The ad agency customarily provides the lyrics for the jingle. The amount charged by the music supplier is two-fold: (1)a creative fee (typically ranging from $1,500 to as much as $15,000 for one 30-second commercial; but if the advertising campaign involves a celebrity artist/songwriter, such as Billy Joel, the creative fees may be in the millions); and (2)production costs (to cover the costs of hiring musicians and studio rental).

The music supplier not only writes the music, but provides the finished master as well. Therefore, the music supplier, as a musician, is entitled to residual royalty payments per SAG and AFTRA union contracts. In addition, music suppliers, as composers and publishers, may receive a small amount of performing royalties from ASCAP/BMI.

## 2) EXISTING SONGS

If an ad agency wishes to use a particular version of a song that is already on a record, they must acquire the rights to use the song by (1)obtaining a master use license from the record company, and (2)obtaining a sync license from the songwriter's publisher.[53] License fees vary greatly depending on such factors as whether the song is to be played on television or radio, the length of the song's use, the song's popularity, whether the use of the song is limited to certain types of products, and how elaborate the arrangement is. For a national commercial, record companies charge between $5,000 and $15,000 to use their master recording of a popular song. Publishers charge upwards of $100,000 for a sync license to use the song itself.[54]

---

[53] The ad agency need not obtain a master use license if it re-records the song; rather, only a sync license is necessary.

[54] If an ad agency wishes to save money, e.g., for a low-budget ad campaign, they may license existing stock music (usually background scores) from a music library or a post-production house. The license fees for such music are generally very low (e.g., $100 or less), with no residuals payable to the songwriters. Such music is usually recorded in nonunion sessions abroad.

# CONCLUSION

Congratulations! You've made it through a lot of difficult information about the deal points and numbers that guide the music business. If we've done our job, you have a better understanding of the music business and are much less likely to get ripped off.

Even if everything we've discussed didn't sink in the first time you read it, it is our hope that you will refer to this book time and time again as a guide to alert you to any "red flags" suggesting that someone might be trying to take advantage of you. Use it to ask questions of lawyers, record company personnel and anyone else in the business you come in contact with. If someone asks you to sign a contract or give up rights that don't seem to line up with the suggested deal points or numbers in this book, don't just sign on the dotted line — call them on it.

Good luck with your music career.

We have compiled this book as an educational tool. Because of the constantly changing laws related to this field, the information presented in this book should not be construed as legal advice, but merely educational information. For advice on any specific questions, please contact an attorney.

# RECOMMENDED READING

The authors would like to acknowledge other outstanding sources of information (apart from those already listed elsewhere) that the reader will benefit from:

Brabec, Jeffrey and Brabec, Todd. *Music, Money, and Success.* New York, NY: Schirmer Books, 1994

Clevo, Jim and Olsen, Eric. *Networking In The Music Industry.* San Diego, CA: Rockpress Publishing Company, 1993.

Dannen, Fredric. *Hit Men.* New York, NY: Vintage Books, 1991.

Halloran, Mark. *The Musician's Business And Legal Guide.* Englewood Cliffs, NJ: Prentice-Hall, Inc., 1996.

Hustwit, Gary. *Getting Radio Airplay.* San Diego, CA: Rockpress Publishing Company, 1994.

Hustwit, Gary. *Releasing An Independent Record.* San Diego, CA: Rockpress Publishing Company, 1995.

Passman, Donald S. *All You Need To Know About The Music Business.* New York, NY: Simon & Schuster, 1997.

Poe, Randy. *Music Publishing: A Songwriter's Guide.* Cincinnati, OH: Writer's Digest Books, 1990.

Shemel, Sidney and Krasilovsky, M. William. *This Business of Music.* New York, NY: Billboard Books, 1995.

Siegel, Alan H. *Breaking In To The Music Business.* New York, NY: Simon & Schuster/Fireside, 1990.

Warner, Jay. *How To Have Your Hit Song Published.* Milwaukee, WI: Hal Leonard Books, 1988.

# ABOUT THE AUTHORS

**David Naggar, Esq.**, 40, practices music law in San Francisco, California. Mr. Naggar graduated Phi Beta Kappa from the University of California at Berkeley in 1978, where he received a Bachelor of Science degree in Business Administration. He received his Juris Doctor from the University of California, at Berkeley (Boalt Hall) School of Law in 1981. Since graduating from law school, Mr. Naggar has, in addition to practicing law, interned in the Creative Department of the music publishing giant, Warner-Chappel. On the lighter side, Mr. Naggar fancies himself a semi-skilled musician, having played drums professionally for many years.

**Jeffrey D. Brandstetter, Esq.**, 37, practices entertainment law in San Francisco, California as a partner in the Law Offices of Brandstetter & Green. He received his Bachelor of Arts degree from Brandeis University in Waltham, Massachusetts, and his Juris Doctor from the University of San Francisco School of Law in San Francisco, California. He is an active member of both California Lawyers for the Arts and the Northern California Songwriters Association. In addition to practicing law, Mr. Brandstetter enjoys playing guitar, windsurfing, skiing and tae kwon do.

Mssrs. Brandstetter and Naggar have counseled and represented an array of clients in the music industry, including artists, songwriters, personal managers, producers, record companies and publishers. The authors can be reached at:

1824 Beach Street
San Francisco, CA 94123

David Naggar
dnaggar@earthlink.net

Jeffrey Brandstetter
sfmusiclaw@earthlink.net